I

Scott Foresman

Accelerating English Language Learning

Authors

Anna Uhl Chamot

Jim Cummins

Carolyn Kessler

J. Michael O'Malley

Lily Wong Fillmore

Consultant

George González

Longman

Illustrations Unless otherwise acknowledged, all illustrations are the property of Scott, Foresman and Company. Page abbreviations are as follows: (T) top, (B) bottom, (L) left, (R) right, (C) center.

Louiise Baker 114; Clare Jett/Jennifer Bolton 126(T)–127(B), 228(T, B); Melissa Turk/Ka Botzis 8–9, 38; Cecile Duray-Bito 78–79(B, C), 80–81(B); Allan Eitzen 136(C); Howard S. Friedman 100, 102(B), 106(B); Steven Edsey/Mike Hagel 7(B), 29(T); Christina Tugeau/Laurie Harden 196–197, 200(L); Richard Salzman/Denise Hilton-Cambell 49–51; Michéle Manasse/Carol Inouye 88–89; Melissa Turk/Susan Johnston-Carlson 28(R); Bob Lange 24, 34, 139(B), 160(R), 176–177, 228(TR); Carol Chislovsky/David Lund 210–213(T); Carol Chislovsky/Peg Magovern 40–41(B), 124–125, 154–155, 210–213(C); Mapping Specialists 56(R), 118(B), 133(B); Carol Chislovsky/Martens & Kiefer 42, 195; Robert Masheris 3(TR); Amnerican Artists/Chuck Passarelli 64–75; Gwen Walters/Gary Phillips 222–223; Deborah Wolfe/Saul Rosenbaum 184(T)–187(T); Carla Simmons 82(B), 110(T), 111(T); Raymond Smith 2, 3(B); Holly Hahn/Steve Snodgrass 46–47; Christina Tugeau/Frank Sofo 35(T), 52; Gwen Walters/Susan Spellman 188–190; Richard Salzman/Wayne Anthony Still 140–143, 192–193; Irmeli Holmberg/Kat thacker 164–171; Gwen Walters/Gary Torrisi 121(TR); Carol Chislovsky/Cathy Trachok 43,48(B), 76, 216–217, 226–227(B); Christina Tugeau/Meryl Treatner 202–209; Vicki Wehrman 152.

Literature 12–23: Reprinted with the permission of Simon & Schuster Books for Young Readers from THE NEWS ABOUT DINOSAURS by Patricia Lauber. Text copyright © 1989 Patricia Lauber. 88–99: "Why the Sea Is Salty," by Gail Sakurai. From JACK AND JILL, Copyright © 1995 by Children's Better Health Institute, Benjamin Franklin Literary & Medical Society, Inc., Indianapolis, Indiana. Used by permission. 144–151: From HILL OF FIRE by Thomas P. Lewis. Text copyright © 1971 by Thomas P. Lewis. Illustrations copyright © 1971 by Joan Sandlin. Reprinted by permission of HarperCollins Publishers. 164–171: "The Tug of War" from THIRTY-THREE MULTICULTURAL TALES TO TELL by Pleasant DeSpain (August House, 1993). Copyright © 1993 by Pleasant DeSpain. Reprinted by permission. 199: Excerpt from SCHOOL DAZE by Louis Philips. 202–209: From IN THE YEAR OF THE BOAR AND JACKIE ROBINSON by Bette Bao Lord. Copyright © 1984 by Bette Bao Lord. Reprinted by permission of HarperCollins Publishers. 226–227: From NEW KIDS ON THE BLOCK by Janet Bode. Copyright © 1989 by Janet Bode. Reprinted by permission of Franklin Watts, Inc.

Poems and Songs 24: "Seismosaurus" from TYRANNOSAURUS WAS A BEAST by Jack Prelutsky. Copyright © 1988 by Jack Prelutsky. Reprinted by permission of Greenwillow Books, a division of William Morrow & Company, Inc. 38: "The Crocodile" from ZOO DOINGS by Jack Prelutsky. Copyright © 1983. Used by permission. 50: "Hey Little Girl" reprinted by permission of Coward-McCann, Inc. from APPLES ON A STICK, text copyright © 1983 by Barbara Michels and Bettye White. 51: "Miss Mary Mack" reprinted by permission of Coward-McCann, Inc. from APPLES ON A STICK, text copyright © 1983 by Barbara Michels and Bettye White. 76: "I Am the Running Girl" from I AM THE RUNNING GIRL by Arnold Adoff. Copyright © 1979. Used by permission. 100: "Shells" from I THOUGHT I HEARD THE CITY by Lilian Moore. Copyright © 1969 by Lilian Moore. Reprinted by permission of Marian Reiner for the author. 114: "Yellow Submarine" words and music by John Lennon and Paul McCartney. Copyright © 1966. Used by permission. 152: "V is for Volcano" from "Puptents and Pebbles: A Nonsense ABC" in LAUGHING TIME.

COLLECTED NONSENSE by William Jay Smith. Copyright © 1990 by William Jay Smith. Reprinted by permission of Farrar, Straus & Giroux, Inc. 172: "There's Motion Everywhere" from THERE'S MOTION EVERYWHERE by John Travers Moore. Copyright © 1970 by John Travers Moore. Reprinted by permission of The University of Virginia Library. 190: "Let's Twist Again," by Kal Mann and Dave Appell. Copyright © 1961 Kalmann Music, Inc. Used by permission. 214: Reprinted with permission of Simon & Schuster Books for Young Readers from IF YOU'RE NOT HERE, PLEASE RAISE YOUR HAND by Kalli Dakos. Text copyright © 1990 Kalli Dakos. 228: "Aprender el inglés/Learning English" by Alberto Ambroggio, translated by Lori M. Carlson. From COOL SALSA edited by Lori M. Carlson. Collection copyright © 1994 by Lori M. Carlson. Reprinted by permission of Henry Holt and Company, Inc.

Photography Unless otherwise acknowledged, all photographs are the property of Scott, Foresman and Company. Page abbreviations are as follows: (T) top, (C) center, (B) bottom, (R) right.

v(t) Fred Fellman/Tony Stone Images; (bl, bc) Superstock, Inc.; **4**(b) William E. Ferguson; (t) Breck P. Kent/Earth Scenes; **5**(b) Smithsonian Institution; **6**(b) William E. Ferguson; (t) E.R.Degginger/Earth Scenes; **7** L.L.T. Rhodes/Earth Scenes; **12–13** © Mark Hallett; **14** © Robert T. Bakker; **15** © Gragory S. Paul; **16** Courtesy of Princeton University; **17** © Douglas Henderson; **18–19, 20** © Gregory S. Paul; **21** Dauglas Henderson/© Collection of Phil Tippett; **22** © John Gurche 1985; **23** © Gragory S. Paul; **26**(b) Michael J. Howell/Superstock, Inc.; (t, cl, dr) Boltin Picture Library; **27**(tr, br) Boltin Picture Library; **29**(t, b) Richard T. Nowitz, **30** Field Museum of Natural History; **32**(t) Superstock, Inc.; (br) Boltin Picture Library; (bl) Archive Photos; **33**(tl, tr) Boltin Picture Library; **35**(b) British Museum; **36** Patrick Landmann/Gamma-Liaison; **37** Barry Iverson/Woodfin Camp & Associates; **40** Jeff Greenburg/PhotoEdit; **41**(b) Westlight; (t) Lawrence Migdale/Tony Stone Images; **48** Tom Dietrich/Tony Stone Images; **49** David Young-Wolff/PhotoEdit; **54** Richard Saker/Allsport USA; **55**(cr) Richard Martin/Agence Vandystadt/Allsport; (b) David Cannon/Allsport USA; (cl) Steve Powell/Allsport USA; (tr) Simon Brut/Allsport USA; (tl) Mike Powell/Allsport USA ; **56**(t) Archeological Museum, Athens/Bridgeman Art Library, London/Superstock, Inc.; **57**(c) Archeological Museum, Florence/Scala/Superstock, Inc.; (t) Stock Montage, Inc.; (b) Granger Collection, New York; **58**(b) Museo Delle Terme, Rome/Superstock, Inc; (c) Granger Collection, New York; (t) D. Strohmeyer/Allsport; **59**(cr) Superstock, Inc.; (bl) Pascal Rondeau/Allsport USA; (br) Allsport USA; (t) Susan Camp/Allsport USA; **60**(t) North Wind Picture Archives; (b) Don Morley/Allsport USA; **61** (t) Reuters/Corbis-Bettmann; (b) Allsport/Hutton Deutsh; **62** Gary Newkirk/Allsport; **78** Micky Gibson/Animals Animals Earth Acenes; **79**(t) Fred Felleman/Tony Stone Images; (b) Superstock, Inc.; **82**(b) Superstock, Inc.; (t) Superstock, Inc.; **83**(tr) Superstock, Inc.; (tl) Superstock, Inc.; (c) Rudie H. Kuiter/Oxford Scientific Films/Animals Animals/Earth Scenes; (b) Peter Parks/Oxford Scientific Films/Animals Animals/Earth Scenes; **102**(r) Superstock, Inc.; (l) Mickey Gibson/Earth Scenes; **103**(bl) Superstock, Inc.; (br) Flip Schulke/Black Star, (t) L.L.T. Rhodes/Earth Scenes; **104**(b) C.C. Lockwood/Earth Scenes; (t) Victoria McCormick/Earth Scenes; **105**(t) Superstock, Inc.; (b) Superstock, Inc.; (c) Animals Animals; **107**(t) Richard Fako/Black Star; **110** Superstock, Inc.; **113** Robert E. Cammrich/Tony Stone Images; **115** Superstock, Inc.; **116**(c) Superstock, Inc.; (l) Superstock, Inc.; (r) Superstock, Inc.; **117**(b) Tony Stone Images; (t) Superstock, Inc.; **118** Superstock, Inc.; **119**(br) Superstock, Inc.; (cb) Metropolitan museum of Art; (t) Library of the University of Edinburgh; (tc) Library of the University of Edinburgh; **120**(b) Superstock, Inc.; **121**(t) Michelle E. Ryan; (b) Robert Freck/Odyssey Productions; **122–123** Superstock, Inc.; **122**(l) William Rockhill Nelson Gallery of Art, Atkins Museum of Fine Arts, Kansas City Missouri; **129**(tl) Library of the University of Edinburgh; (bl) Library of the University of Edinburgh; **130**(b) Ralph Perry/Balck Star; **130–131** (background) L. Mason/Balck Star; **131**(b) Superstock, Inc.; (t) Superstock, Inc.; **132** ACME/Corbis-Bettmann; **133** Pierre Vauthey/Sygma; **134**(t) Alessandra Qauranta/Black Star; **136**(b) © 1993 Achim Sperber/black Star; **137**(bl) Scala/Art Resource; (bc, br) Scala/Art Resource; **138**(t, b), **153, 174**(b), **174–175** Superstock, Inc.; **175**(t) Steve Smith/Westlight; (b) Superstock, Inc.; **182–183** Terry Barner/Unicorn Stock Photos; **184** Russell R. Grundke/Unicorn Stock Photos; **184, 186** Superstock, Inc.; **187** Robert Condau/Westlight; **191** Superstock, Inc.; **202** AP/Wide World; **210** Courtesy of Sayo Yamaguchi; **218** UPI/Corbis-Bettman; **221, 222** AP/Wide World; (t) Museum of Fine Arts, Boston.

CONSULTANTS

Sandra H. Bible
Elementary ESL Teacher
Shawnee Mission School District
Shawnee Mission, Kansas

Anaida Colón-Muñiz, Ed.D.
Director of English Language
Development
and Bilingual Education
Santa Ana Unified School District
Santa Ana, California

Debbie Corkey-Corber
Educational Consultant
Williamsburg, Virginia

Barbara Crandall
Carol Baranyi
Ilean Zamlut
ESOL Teachers
Lake Park Elementary School
Palm Beach County, Florida

Lily Pham Dam
Instructional Specialist
Dallas Independent School District
Dallas, Texas

María Delgado
Milwaukee Public Schools
Milwaukee, Wisconsin

Dr. M. Viramontes de Marín
Chair, Department of Education and
Liberal Studies at the National
Hispanic University
San Jose, California

Virginia Hansen
ESOL Resource Teacher
Palm Beach County, Florida

Tim Hart
Supervisor of English as a Second
Language
Wake County
Releigh, North Carolina

Lilian I. Jezik
Bilingual Resource Teacher
Corona-Norco Unified School District
Norco, California

Helen L. Lin
Chairman, Education Program
Multicultural Arts Council of
Orange County, California
Formerly ESL Lab Director,
Kansas City, Kansas Schools

Justine McDonough
Trish Lirio
Sheree Di Donato
Jupiter Elementary School
West Palm Beach, Florida

Teresa Montaña
United Teachers Los Angeles
Los Angeles, California

Loriana M. Novoa, Ed.D.
Research and Evaluation Consultants
Miami, Florida

Beatrice Palls
ESOL and Foreign Language
Supervisor
Pasco County, Florida

Rosa María Peña
Austin Independent School District
Austin, Texas

Alice Quarles
Assistant Principal
Fairlawn Elementary School
Dade County, Florida

Thuy Pham-Remmele
ESL/Bilingual K–12 Specialist
Madison Metropolitan School District
Madison, Wisconsin

Jacqueline J. Servi Margis
ESL and Foreign Language
Curriculum Specialist
Milwaukee Public Schools
Milwaukee, Wisconsin

Carmen Sorondo
Supervisor, ESOL, K–12
Hillsborough County, Florida

Susan C. VanLeuven
Poudre R-1 School District
Fort Collins, Colorado

Rosaura Villaseñor
(Educator)
Norwalk, California

Cheryl Wilkinson
J. O. Davis Elementary School
Irving Independent School District
Irving, Texas

Phyllis I. Ziegler
ESL/Bilingual Consultant
New York, New York

TABLE OF CONTENTS

UNIT 1 • IDEAS IN CONFLICT

Digging Up the Past 2

CHAPTER 1 **Digging Up Fossils** 4
The News About Dinosaurs by Patricia Lauber
"Seismosaurus" by Jack Prelutsky

CHAPTER 2 **Digging Up Ancient Objects** 26
"The Crocodile" by Jack Prelutsky

UNIT 2 • CHALLENGES

Good Sports 40

CHAPTER 3 **Types of Fitness** 42
"Take Me Out to the Ball Game" a song

CHAPTER 4 **Olympic Challenges** 54
Atalanta and the Golden Apples retold
by Margot Biersdorf
"I Am the Running Girl" by Arnold Adoff

UNIT 3 • ENVIRONMENT

Oceans 79

CHAPTER 5 **Life Underwater** 80
Why the Sea is Salty retold by Gail Sakurai
"Shells" by Lilian Moore

CHAPTER 6 **Taking Care of the Oceans** 102
"Yellow Submarine" a song by John Lennon
and Paul McCartney

UNIT 4 • JUSTICE

The Ancient Romans . . . 116

CHAPTER 7 The Roman Empire 118
Roman Recipes

CHAPTER 8 Volcanoes in History 130
An Ancient Roman Myth: The God Vulcan
Hill of Fire by Thomas P. Lewis
"V is for Volcano" by William Jay Smith

UNIT 5 • RELATIONSHIPS

The Physics of Fun 154

CHAPTER 9 What Makes Things Move? . . . 156
The Tug of War by Pleasant DeSpain
"There's Motion Everywhere" by John Travers
   Moore

CHAPTER 10 Physics of Roller Coasters 174
"Let's Twist Again" a song by Kal Mann

UNIT 6 • CHANGE

Dealing with Change . . .192

CHAPTER 11 Handling Stress 194
In the Year of the Boar and Jackie Robinson
   by Bette Bao Lord
Schools in Japan and the United States
   by Sayo Yamaguchi
"You Can Do Better" by Kalli Dakos

CHAPTER 12 Getting Information 216
"Aprender el inglés" by Luis Albero Amroggio
"Learning English" translated by Lori M. Carlson

Writer's Workshop 230

Digging Up the Past

Tell what you know.

What do you think these dinosaurs were like?

Were they fast or slow?

Did they eat meat or plants?

Ankylosaur ▶

▼ Hadrosaur

▼ Velociraptor

◀ Triceratops

▼ Deinonychus

▲ Tyrannosaurus rex

Why are people
interested in dinosaurs?

3

Digging Up Fossils

How do scientists learn about dinosaurs?

Dinosaurs died millions of years ago. After millions of years, the hard parts of the animals, like bones and teeth, turned into stone. They became **fossils.**

Scientists study fossil bones. They put an animal's bones together to make a skeleton. They can tell how tall the animal was. They can tell how fast the animal walked.

Scientists study fossil teeth too. They can tell what the animal ate. Meat-eaters had sharp teeth. Plant-eaters had flat teeth.

Talk About It

What parts of an animal can become fossils? What parts of an animal can't become fossils?

Dinosaur Fossils

This dinosaur's bones turned into fossils.
Scientists put the fossil bones together to
make a skeleton.

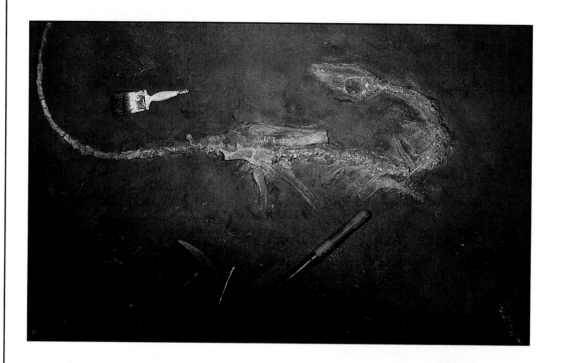

A dinosaur laid eggs in this nest.
The eggs and baby dinosaurs
turned into fossils. Scientists
study the fossils.

A dinosaur walked through mud and left these footprints. The mud turned into stone. Scientists study the footprints.

Dinosaur teeth turned into fossils. Scientists study the dinosaur teeth.

? Think About It

What kinds of fossils have scientists found? What can scientists learn about dinosaurs from each kind of fossil?

When did dinosaurs live?

Scientists divide history into long numbers of years called **eras.** Eras are divided into **periods.**

The chart shows the era and periods when dinosaurs lived.

Are the oldest events at the top or the bottom of the chart?

Era	Period	
Cenozoic	Quaternary	2 million years ago to present
	Tertiary	63 to 2 million years ago
Mesozoic	Cretaceous	138 million to 63 million years ago
	Jurassic	205 to 138 million years ago
	Triassic	240 to 205 million years ago

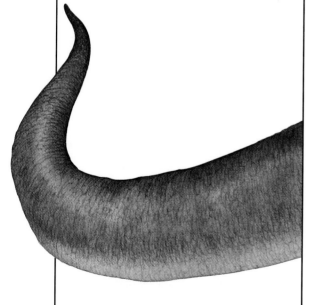

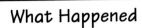

What Happened

Humans appeared.

Mammals like horses and elephants appeared.

Dinosaurs died out 63 million years ago.
The last new dinosaurs appeared 68 million years ago.

Tyrannosaurus
(40 feet or 12 meters long)

Triceratops
(25 feet or 7.6 meters long)

Flowering plants appeared.

Allosaurus
(36 feet or 11 meters long)

Brachiosaurus
(75 feet or 23 meters
long) appeared.

Birds appeared.

First dinosaurs appeared.

Plateosaurus
(20 feet or 6 meters long)

Anchisaurus
(8 feet or 2.5 meters long)

First mammals appeared.

Talk About It

Did flowering plants appear before or after the first birds?

Did mammals appear before or after the dinosaurs died out?

How long had dinosaurs been dead before humans appeared?

Make more questions about the chart. Ask a partner.

You can make fossils.

Things You Need

🐚 shell   ⬜ petroleum jelly   📦 plaster of Paris   💧 water

🫙 jar   🥄 plastic spoon   🧂 clay

To make a mold:

1. Make the clay into a circle.

2. Cover the seashell with petroleum jelly. Cover the clay with petroleum jelly.

3. Press the outside of the seashell into the clay.

4. Remove the shell from the clay.

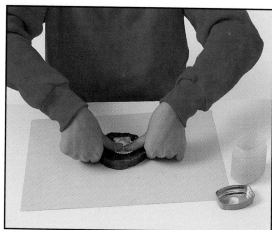

To make a cast:

1. Mix the plaster of Paris with water.

2. Pour the plaster into the mold.

3. Let the plaster dry overnight.

4. Remove the plaster from the clay.

My Record

This is my fossil.

It is like a dinosaur fossil because

▽ **Write About It**

Some dinosaur fossils are molds and some are casts. Draw one of your fossils. How is it like a dinosaur fossil?

The News About Dinosaurs

by Patricia Lauber

Strategy Tip
Read On to Get Meaning
The author uses the word *reptile*. Read on to find examples of reptiles. What examples of reptiles does the author give?

Dinosaurs were discovered in the early 1800s. Until then, no one had even guessed that once there were dinosaurs.

Scientists studied the big teeth and bones they had found. They wondered what kind of animals these belonged to. Finally they decided the animals were reptiles—relatives of today's crocodiles, turtles, snakes, and lizards. In 1841 the animals were named *dinosaurs*, meaning "terrible lizards."

Dinosaur hunters dug for bones. They found giant dinosaurs, dinosaurs the size of chickens, and many in-between sizes. They gave each kind a name. They fitted bones together and made skeletons. After a hundred or more years, this work seemed to be ending. Scientists began to think they had discovered nearly every kind of dinosaur that ever walked the earth.

▼ *Mamenchisaurus* was a giant plant-eating dinosaur, 72 feet long. Its 33-foot neck is the longest of any known animal. The dinosaur is named for the place in China where it was found.

Strategy Tip
Read to Understand the Big Idea
Don't try to remember or pronounce all the dinosaurs' names. Read to find out what ideas scientists have about dinosaurs.

THE NEWS IS:

The work was far from finished. Today new kinds of dinosaurs are found all the time. And scientists think there must be hundreds more that they haven't discovered yet. Four of the new kinds they have found are *Baryonyx*, *Mamenchisaurus*, *Deinonychus*, and *Nanotyrannus*.

▼ *Nanotyrannus* was a pygmy tyrannosaur, a small relative of *Tyrannosaurus rex*. Its name means "pygmy tyrant." This small meat-eating dinosaur looked like its big relative but was only one-tenth as heavy and one-third as long—it weighed about 1,000 pounds and was 17 feet long. *Nanotyrannus* was discovered in a museum, where it had earlier been mistaken for another meat-eater, a gorgosaur, also known as *Albertosaurus*. Here its jaws are about to close on a smaller dinosaur.

▲ *Deinonychus* was found in Montana. It was fairly small, about 9 feet long, and walked on its hind legs. Each hind foot had a big claw, shaped like a curved sword. The dinosaur's name means "terrible claw." Like other meat-eaters, *Deinonychus* spent much of its time resting or sleeping and digesting its last meal. This pair has just awakened, hungry and ready to hunt.

Language Tip
Synonyms
Waddling and dragging mean "moving slowly."

Strategy Tip
Predict
Here you read that the old idea was that dinosaurs were slow and clumsy. What will the new idea about dinosaurs be?

Most reptiles walk with their knees bent and their feet wide apart. Scientists used to think dinosaurs must have walked the same way. They pictured dinosaurs as slow and clumsy, waddling along with their tails dragging on the ground. So that was how dinosaurs were made to look in books and museums.

▲ For many years, people thought of dinosaurs as slow-moving and slow-witted. That is how they appear in this 1870s painting by Benjamin Waterhouse Hawkins. He was the first artist to work closely with scientists who were studying dinosaurs.

THE NEWS IS:

Dinosaurs didn't look like that at all. They were good walkers. They held their tails up. And many kinds were quick and nimble. Today's scientists have learned this by studying dinosaur footprints.

Strategy Tip
Synonyms
When you read, look for words that mean the same.
quick—nimble
mud—wet sand
footprints—tracks

▼ *Camarasaurs* (foreground) and *camptosaurs* are crossing a recently flooded area and leaving footprints. Preserved in rock, such tracks have revealed much about dinosaurs.

When dinosaurs walked in mud or wet sand, they left footprints. Most of these tracks washed or oozed away. But in some places the tracks hardened. Later they were buried under mud or sand that turned to rock. The tracks were preserved in the rock—they became fossils.

▼ Today dinosaurs are shown as lively and active. These huge, horned plant-eaters are driving off *Albertosaurus,* a fierce meat-eater.

Tracks show that dinosaurs walked in long, easy strides. Their legs and feet were under their bodies, not out to the side. Their bodies were high off the ground. Big plant-eaters walked at 3 or 4 miles an hour. Some small meat-eaters could run as fast as 35 or 40 miles an hour.

▼ At least some dinosaurs could swim. *Apatosaurus* has tried to escape a pack of *Allosaurus* by taking to the water—but the meat-eaters can swim, too.

▶ A splash of color would call attention to the spiny neck frill of this horned dinosaur, which may have frightened meat-eaters.

All of today's reptiles are cold-blooded. Their bodies do not make much heat. To be active, reptiles need an outside source of heat—sunlight, warm air, sun-warmed water. When reptiles are cool, they are sluggish and slow-moving.

Mammals and birds are warm-blooded. They make their own heat, and they can be active by day or by night, in warm weather or in cool. They have much more energy than reptiles do and can stay active for hours at a time.

Scientists long thought that dinosaurs, like today's reptiles, were cold-blooded animals.

Strategy Tip
Antonyms
When you read, look for words that mean the opposite.
warm—cool
active—sluggish

THE NEWS IS:

Some dinosaurs may have been warm-blooded. *Deinonychus*—"terrible claw"—is one of those dinosaurs.

Deinonychus was fairly small. It had the sharp teeth of a meat-eater, hands shaped for grasping prey, and powerful hind legs. It also had a huge, curved claw on one toe of each hind foot. This was a claw shaped for ripping and slashing.

Language Tip
Vocabulary
Animals that are hunted and eaten are called *prey*. An animal's *hind legs* are its back legs.

▼ Three *Deinonychus* work together to bring down *Iguanodon,* which was too old or too sick to defend itself with its thumb spike or tail.

To attack, *Deinonychus* must have stood on one hind foot and slashed with the other. Or it must have leaped and attacked with both hind feet. Today's reptiles are not nimble enough to do anything like that. And as cold-blooded animals, they do not have the energy to attack that way. Warm-blooded animals do. That is why some scientists think *Deinonychus* must have been a warm-blooded dinosaur. They also think that many of the small, meat-eating dinosaurs were warm-blooded.

▲ *Deinonychus* and other small meat-eaters may have had feathers.

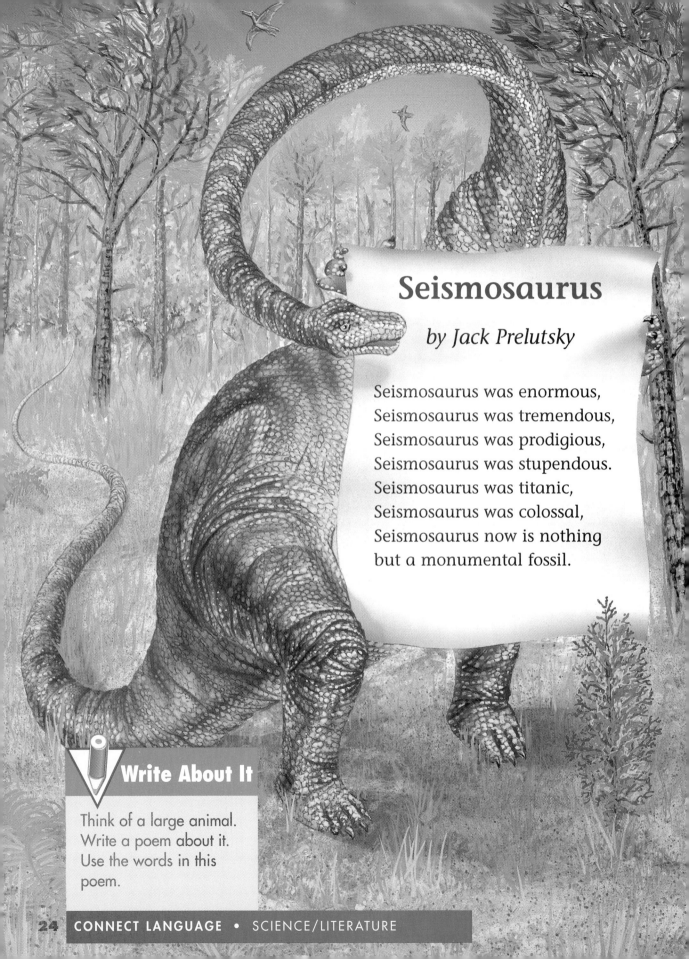

Seismosaurus

by Jack Prelutsky

Seismosaurus was enormous,
Seismosaurus was tremendous,
Seismosaurus was prodigious,
Seismosaurus was stupendous.
Seismosaurus was titanic,
Seismosaurus was colossal,
Seismosaurus now is nothing
but a monumental fossil.

Write About It

Think of a large animal.
Write a poem about it.
Use the words in this
poem.

Tell what you learned.

1. What are fossils? What parts of animals become fossils?

2. Think of scientists' ideas about dinosaurs. Make a chart.

Old Ideas	New Ideas
Scientists know about every kind of dinosaur.	
Dinosaurs moved slowly.	
Dinosaurs were cold-blooded.	

3. What was the most interesting thing you learned about dinosaurs? Why do you think it's interesting?

Digging Up Ancient Objects

Tell what you know.

The ancient Egyptians made these objects. What do you think they used them for?

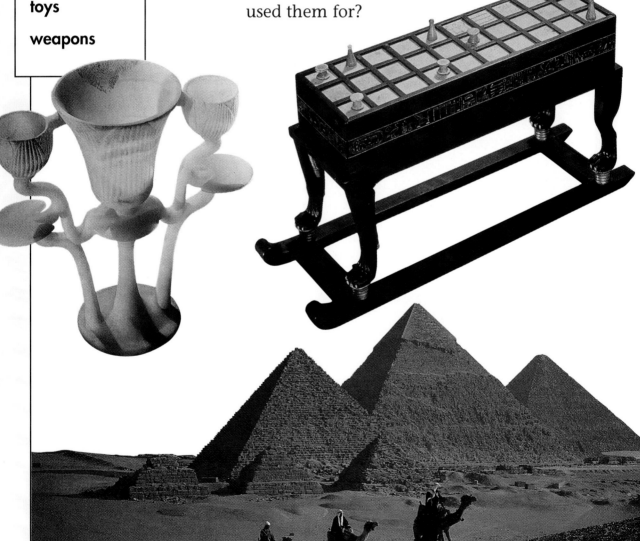

Talk About It

How was life the same for ancient Egyptians as for people today?

How was life different for ancient Egyptians than for people today?

The Ancient Egyptians

The ancient Egyptians lived more than 4,000 years ago. They lived in Africa, in the Nile River Valley. Most Egyptians were farmers. Others were doctors, priests, artists, and builders. They were ruled by kings called **pharaohs.**

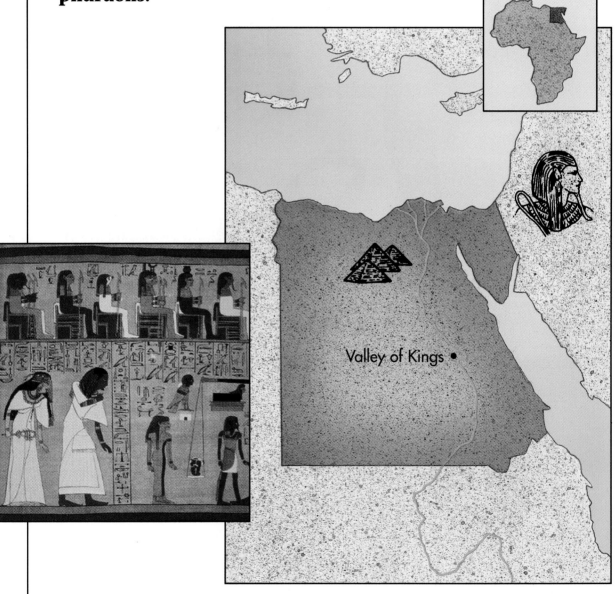

Valley of Kings •

Archaeologists are scientists who study about ancient people. Archaeologists have studied the ancient Egyptians for about two hundred years. They have studied their jewelry, furniture, clothing, weapons, toys, and other **artifacts.**

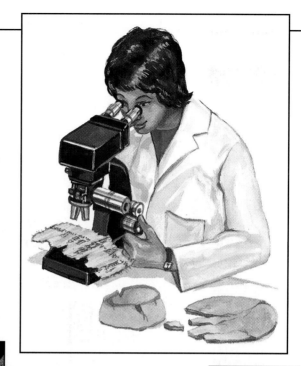

Word Bank

dig

explore

find

photograph

read

study

Talk About It

How do archaeologists learn about the past?

The Pharaohs' Tombs

Ancient Egyptians believed that their spirits lived after their bodies died. The Egyptians believed that they needed their bodies in the spirit world. They preserved dead bodies as **mummies.**

The Egyptians believed that they needed things from the earth in the spirit world. They filled their tombs with useful and precious artifacts.

Mummies were preserved with special oils and wrapped with special cloth.

Some pharaohs were buried in tombs that were hidden in huge **pyramids.** They filled the tombs with gold, jewelry, clothes, toys, furniture, and other precious things. But robbers found the tombs and stole the precious artifacts.

When archaeologists started studying the ancient Egyptians, most of the artifacts from the tombs had disappeared.

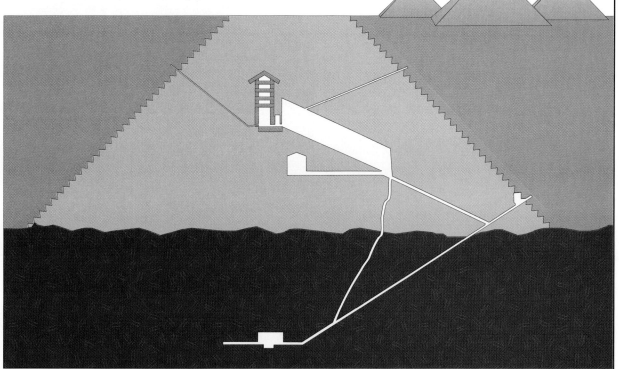

The tomb was in the middle of the pyramid. Tunnels went from the tomb to the outside. When the tomb was finished, the tunnels were filled with rocks.

Write About It

Make a list of things we think of as precious today. Why do we think of these things as precious?

King Tut's Tomb

King Tut lived more than 3,300 years ago. He became king of Egypt when he was 9 years old. He died when he was 18 years old. He lived a short life, but King Tut is one of the most famous pharaohs of all.

In 1922, an archaeologist named Howard Carter discovered King Tut's tomb in the Valley of the Kings.

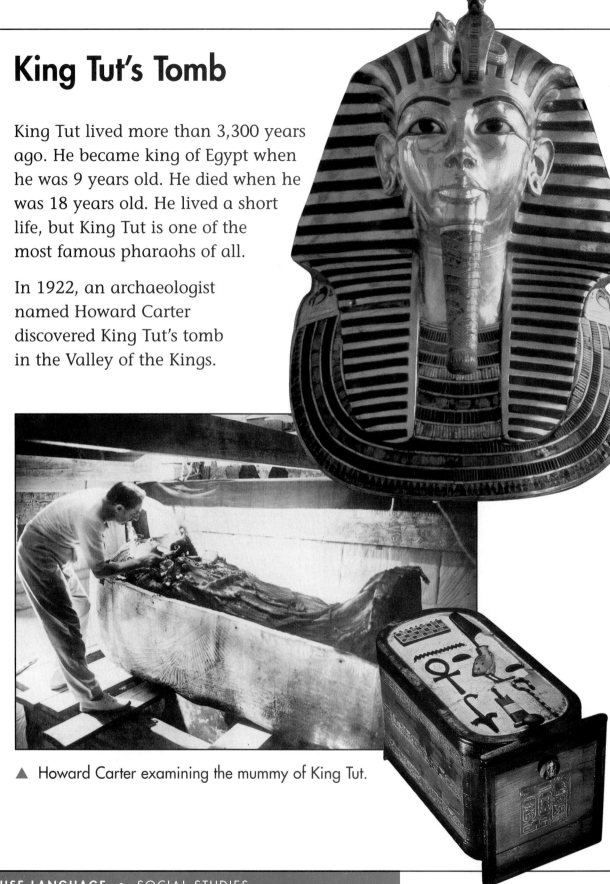

▲ Howard Carter examining the mummy of King Tut.

King Tut's tomb had not been robbed. It contained many precious artifacts. It even contained the mummy of King Tut.

The tomb contained gold, jewelry, furniture, toys, games, weapons, food, and other things. Archaeologists have studied these artifacts and have learned a lot about the ancient Egyptians.

Try It Out

What could people in the future learn about you by studying your clothes, furniture, games, and other things? Put five or six objects that are precious to you in a box. Tell a partner why they are precious.

Hieroglyphics

The ancient Egyptians used a kind of picture writing called **hieroglyphics.** They wrote in hieroglyphics on the walls of their tombs.

After a time, people forgot how to read hieroglyphics. For 1,000 years, no one in the world could read hieroglyphics.

tree

sky

eye

chair

door

weapons

sword

water

star

Then in 1799, a soldier found a rock called the Rosetta Stone. There was writing on the Rosetta Stone in three different languages. All three languages said the same thing. One of the languages was hieroglyphics.

After almost 25 years, archaeologists learned how to read the hieroglyphics. Now they could read about the lives of the ancient Egyptians.

Talk About It

What other languages besides English can you read?

How are the written forms of these languages like English? How are they different?

New Discovery in Egypt Announced

Egypt, 1995—
American archaeologist Kent Weeks has discovered a tomb in Egypt's Valley of the Kings. Most archaeologists believed that all the important tombs there had been discovered.

Weeks disagreed, and today the world knows he was correct.

In 1820, archaeologists found a large room in the Valley of the Kings, but they did not think it was important. In 1988, Weeks decided to explore it.

Weeks and his team explored for seven summers. Finally they found a door. Behind the door, they found many more rooms. They had found a large tomb!

Hieroglyphics in the rooms say that several sons of the pharaoh Ramses II were buried in the tomb about 3,000 years ago.

Long ago robbers found the tomb and stole many objects. However, Weeks hopes to find many artifacts as he explores the tomb.

▲ A statue of the god Osiris from the tomb

Think About It

How have ideas about ancient peoples changed?

How did Weeks show that other archaeologists were wrong?

Crocodiles have lived on earth for millions of years.
Many crocodiles live in the Nile River in Egypt.

The Crocodile

by Jack Prelutsky

Beware the crafty crocodile
who beckons you with clever smile
to join him in the river Nile
and swim with him a little while.

His smile is not a friendly smile,
it springs from his dishonest guile
and treacherous reptilian style.
Beware the crafty crocodile.

Talk About It

Would you get friendly
with a crocodile? Why
or why not?

Tell what you learned.

1. How have archaeologists learned about ancient Egypt?

2. Do you think that archaeologists should keep looking for even more tombs in the Valley of the Kings? Why or why not?

3. You are an archaeologist working in Egypt. What artifact would you most like to find? Why?

Good Sports

Word Bank

do
gymnastics
jog
play softball
run
swim
walk

Tell what you know.

What is fitness?

What are some ways to get fit?

Talk About It

What kinds of exercises do you do? What kinds of sports do you play?

Who should be concerned about fitness?

Types of Fitness

How fit are you?

Physical fitness is important for good health. When you are physically fit, your body is in good condition. When you are healthy, your body lets you do the things you want to do and need to do.

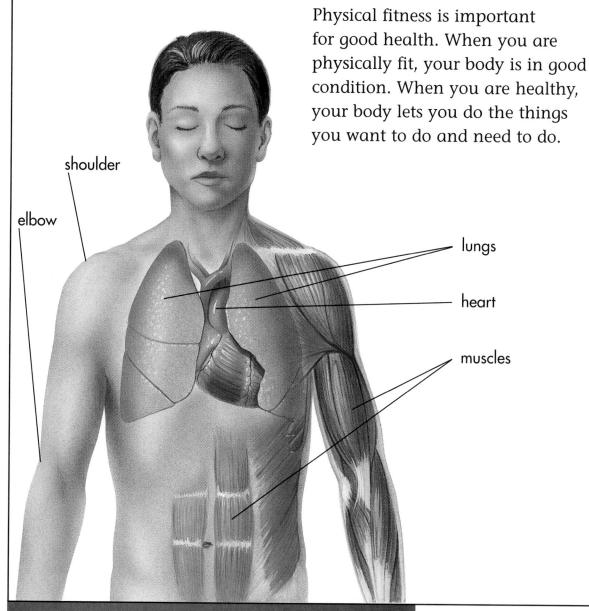

shoulder

elbow

lungs

heart

muscles

Five different kinds of fitness are important for good health.

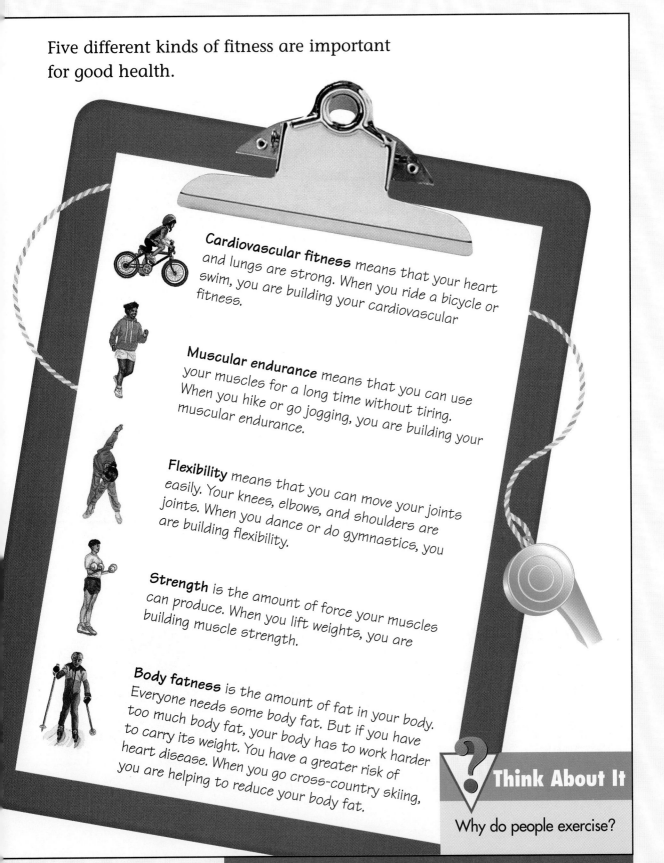

Cardiovascular fitness means that your heart and lungs are strong. When you ride a bicycle or swim, you are building your cardiovascular fitness.

Muscular endurance means that you can use your muscles for a long time without tiring. When you hike or go jogging, you are building your muscular endurance.

Flexibility means that you can move your joints easily. Your knees, elbows, and shoulders are joints. When you dance or do gymnastics, you are building flexibility.

Strength is the amount of force your muscles can produce. When you lift weights, you are building muscle strength.

Body fatness is the amount of fat in your body. Everyone needs some body fat. But if you have too much body fat, your body has to work harder to carry its weight. You have a greater risk of heart disease. When you go cross-country skiing, you are helping to reduce your body fat.

? Think About It

Why do people exercise?

Steps to Fitness

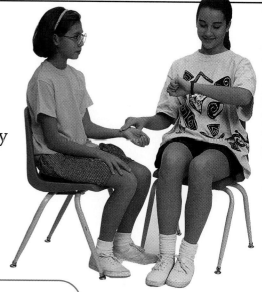

Test your cardiovascular fitness.

Cardiovascular fitness increases your energy level. It helps you stay active for longer periods of time without tiring.

Do this activity to test your cardiovascular fitness.

Things You Need

  a watch or clock with a second hand, or a stopwatch

1. Run in place for 1 minute. Take 2 steps each seconds. This is 120 steps in all.

2. Rest for 1 minute.

3. Feel your pulse. Count your heart rate for 30 seconds.

If you are fit, you will count fewer than 75 heartbeats.

Do an aerobic exercise.

Many people do **aerobic exercises** to build cardiovascular fitness. Your heart is a muscle. Aerobics help exercise your heart.

Read the directions for Step Hop and try it.

1. On count 1, step forward with your right foot.

2. On count 2, step forward with your left foot.

3. On count 3, step forward with your right foot.

4. On count 4, hop on your right foot, kick with your left leg, and clap your hands.

5. Repeat the four counts, but start with your left foot.

6. Do the exercise quickly in time with music.

Talk About It

What other exercises do you know? Show them and explain how to do them.

Make a fitness plan.

To be fit, you must exercise at least

- 3 times a week

- 20 minutes each time

The activities on the chart are good activities to do all your life. Each activity helps to build different kinds of fitness. The chart tells which kind of fitness goes with each activity.

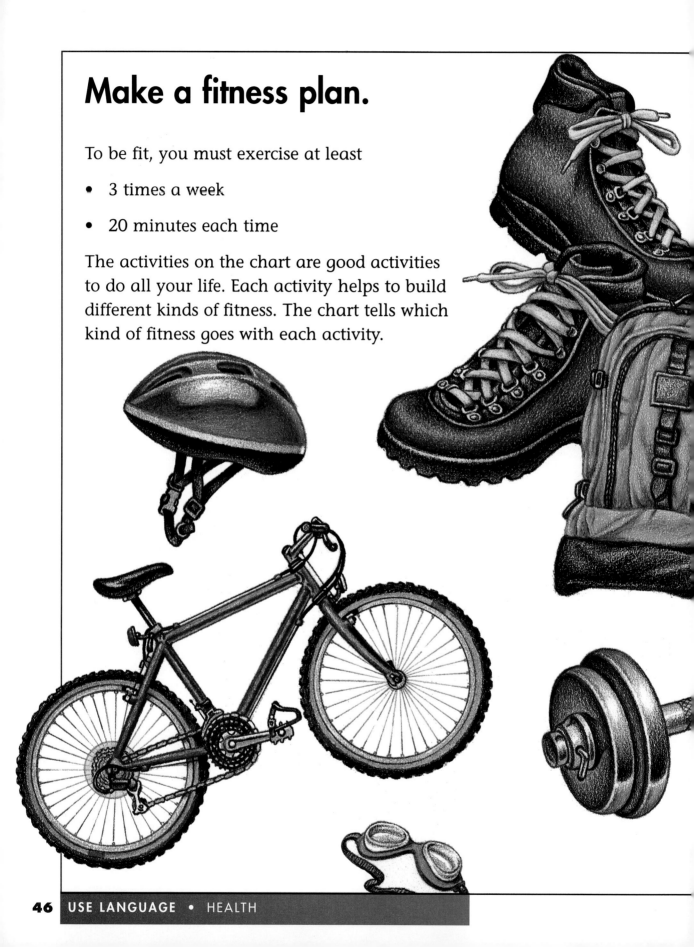

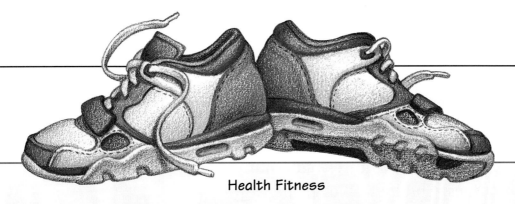

Health Fitness

Physical Activities	Builds Cardiovascular Fitness	Builds Strength	Builds Muscular Endurance	Builds Flexibility	Helps Control Body Fatness
Bicycling	excellent	fair	good	poor	excellent
Dance, Aerobic	excellent	fair	good	good	excellent
Gymnastics	fair	excellent	excellent	excellent	fair
Hiking	good	fair/good	excellent	fair	good
Jogging	excellent	poor	good	poor	excellent
Judo/Karate	poor	fair	fair	fair	poor
Roller Skating	fair/good	poor	fair	poor	fair/good
Swimming	excellent	fair	good	fair	excellent
Weight Lifting	poor	excellent	good	poor	fair

 Write About It

List the physical activities you do. Write how often you do them. Next to each, write the kind of fitness it helps to build.

Look at your list. Is there one fitness area you need to improve? Plan an activity or exercise that will help build that kind of fitness. Decide how often you will do the activity and when you will do it.

Games from Many Cultures

People from different cultures play many similar games. Children all over the world play tag. Tag is a game in which players chase each other and try to tag, or touch, another player.

Beware the Antelope

In Central Africa, tag is called "Beware of the Antelope." The leader, or antelope, chases and tags other players. Then they, too, become antelopes. The game continues until everyone has been tagged.

Catch the Dragon's Tail

In China, children play a kind of tag called "Catch the Dragon's Tail." The leader, or dragon, is at the head of a line. The leader tries to tag the tail, or last person in line.

Bell in the Steeple

In Russia, children play tag with a bell. The game is called "Bell in the Steeple." A "guard" stands in a small square and holds a box. The other players walk around the guard and pass a bell from one to another. When the guard claps, the player with the bell puts it into the guard's box. The other players chase the guard and try to get the bell.

GUARD'S SQUARE

Talk About It

Have you ever played a game like tag? What were the rules?

Jump Rope Rhymes

You have probably seen children jumping rope. As they jump, the children sing rhymes for fun and to keep the rhythm of the jumping. Here are some rhymes.

Hey little girl with dippity do
Your mom's got the measles
And your daddy does too
Take a ABCDEFG
Take a HIJKLMNOP
Take a booster shot
Take a booster shot
And freeze

Miss Mary Mack Mack Mack
All dressed in black black black
With silver buttons buttons buttons
All down her back back back
She asked her mother mother mother
For fifteen cents cents cents
To see the elephant elephant elephant
Jump the fence fence fence
He jumped so high high high
He touched the sky sky sky
And never came back
'Til the fourth of July-ly-ly

Try It Out

Jump by yourself with
a short rope. How
many jumps can you
do in a row?

Take Me Out To The Ball Game

Take me out to the ball game,
Take me out to the crowd,
Buy me some peanuts and Cracker Jack,
I don't care if I ever get back.
So it's root, root, root for the home team,
If they don't win it's a shame,
For it's one, two, three strikes, "You're out!"
At the old ball game.

Talk About It

Baseball is a popular game in this country. What sports were popular in the country you or your family came from?

Tell what you learned.

1. Why is it important to be physically fit? Why is cardiovascular fitness so important?

2. Tell about two exercises you do. How do they help you keep fit?

3. Tell about one new thing you learned about fitness.

CHAPTER 4

Olympic Challenges

Word Bank

baseball

diving

speed skating

track and field

weight lifting

Tell what you know.

What are the Olympics?

What sports are in the Olympics?

Which Olympic athletes do you know about?

What sports skills do Olympic athletes need?

◄ Balance

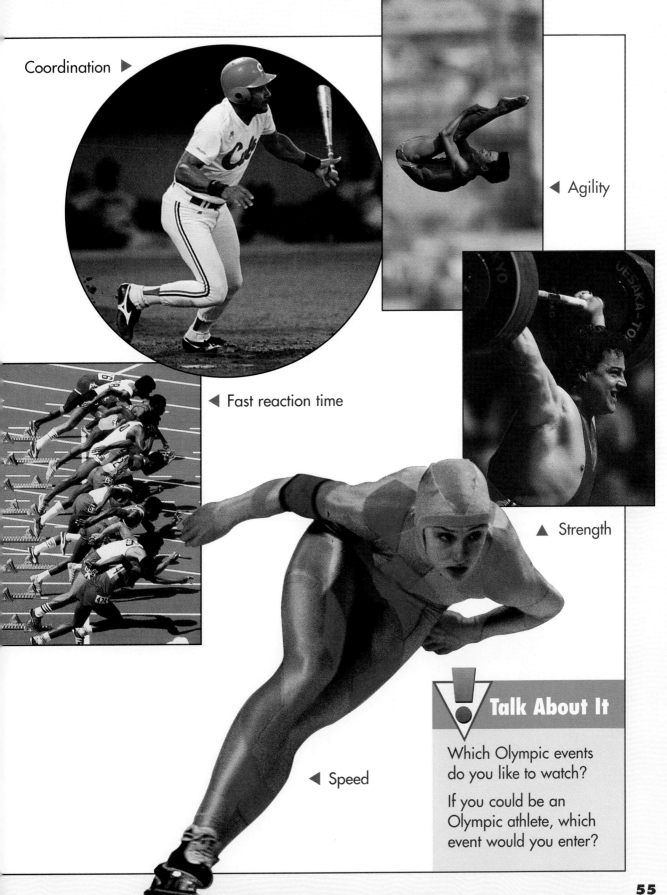

Coordination ▶

◀ Agility

◀ Fast reaction time

▲ Strength

◀ Speed

Talk About It

Which Olympic events do you like to watch?

If you could be an Olympic athlete, which event would you enter?

The Olympic Games

The Olympic Games began in ancient Greece about 2,700 years ago. Every four years, athletes from Greek cities went to Olympia. At Olympia, they competed in sports to honor the god, Zeus.

The Olympic Games were very important to the Greeks. Armies even stopped fighting so the soldiers could compete. Many Olympic events tested skills that were important for soldiers, such as wrestling, throwing the javelin, or racing chariots.

Winners received only a crown of leaves for a prize. But winners became heroes in their cities. They brought fame and honor to their cities because people thought a city with many Olympic heroes was a strong city.

The Olympic Games became famous in other countries. People from other places went to see the games, but only Greek athletes could compete. Foreigners could watch, but they could not compete.

? **Think About It**

In modern Olympics, we count how many medals each country wins. Why?

Are sports important to you? Which ones? Why?

Compare the games.

The modern Olympic Games are similar to the ancient Olympic Games in many ways.

- Athletes in ancient games competed in wrestling, foot races, discus throwing, javelin throwing, and long jumping. Athletes in modern games compete in the same events.

- Winning athletes in the ancient games became heroes. Winning athletes still bring honor and fame to their countries.

The ancient games were different from the modern games in many ways.

- The ancient games included music and speaking contests.

- The ancient games originally took place on one day. Over the years they grew to five days.

- The first ancient games had only one foot race about 200 meters long.

The modern Olympic Games are different from the ancient games in many ways.

- The winners in today's games receive medals, not crowns of leaves.

- There are summer and winter games and many more events. There are many team sports such as basketball and volleyball.

- Today both men and women compete in the games. People from all over the world take part.

- There are events for people with disabilities.

▲ Modern Olympic medal

Talk About It

How would the modern games be different if athletes came from just one country? What are the good things about international games?

Interesting "Firsts"

At each Olympic Games, some winning athletes capture the attention of the world.

The first modern Olympic Games were held in ▶ Greece in 1896. The first event was the triple jump. James Connolly of the United States won this event by jumping 13.71 meters.

▲ At the 1976 Games in Montreal, Canada, Nadia Comaneci of Romania won her place among the firsts for her gymnastic performances. In all Olympic history, no one had earned a perfect 10 from the judges. Nadia earned seven perfect 10's for her performances in Montreal.

Jamaica has no snow. But in 1988 a team from Jamaica wanted to enter the bobsled event during the Winter Olympics in Calgary, Canada. Some people thought that they were not taking a skillful sport seriously. But the team learned to deal with snow and cold weather. They passed the test that allowed them to take part in the Olympics. It was the first time anyone from Jamaica had competed in the winter games.

▲ The marathon is the longest foot race of all. It covers 42,195 meters—over 26 miles! In Rome in 1960, Ethiopian Abebe Bikila became the first African to win the race. He completed it in 2 hours, 15 minutes, and 16.2 seconds. He was also the first runner to run barefoot.

? Think About It

What do you think these athletes did to prepare for their "firsts"?

Who is the fastest?

Speed is important for winning gold medals in some Olympic contests. Here are some speed figures from recent Olympics.

Which athlete do you think was the fastest? Make a guess. List the athletes in order from slowest to fastest.

Athlete	Event	Speed
Linford Christie Great Britain	100-meter dash Men's track	9.96 seconds
William Tanui Kenya	800-meter run Men's track	1 minute 43.66 seconds (103.66 seconds)
Dieter Baumann Germany	5,000-meter run Men's track	13 minutes 12.52 seconds (792.52 seconds)
Zhuang Yong China	100-meter freestyle Women's swimming	54.64 seconds
Janet Evans United States	800-meter freestyle Women's swimming	8 minutes 25.52 seconds (505.52 seconds)
Alexander Golubev Russia	500-meter race Men's speed skating (ice)	36.33 seconds
Johann Olav Koss Norway	5,000-meter race Men's speed skating (ice)	6 minutes 34.96 seconds (394.96 seconds)

Now find how fast each person was moving. Figure the meters per second by dividing each athlete's time into the number of meters he or she covered.

Make a chart showing distance, time, and meters per second for each one.

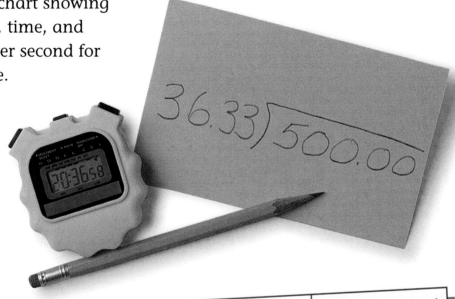

Event	Distance	Time	Meters per Second
Men's track	100 meters	9.96 seconds	10.04 meters

Write About It

In which events do athletes travel at the fastest speeds? Is there a relationship between the length of an event and speed?

Atalanta and the Golden Apples: A Greek Myth

Retold by Margot Biersdorf

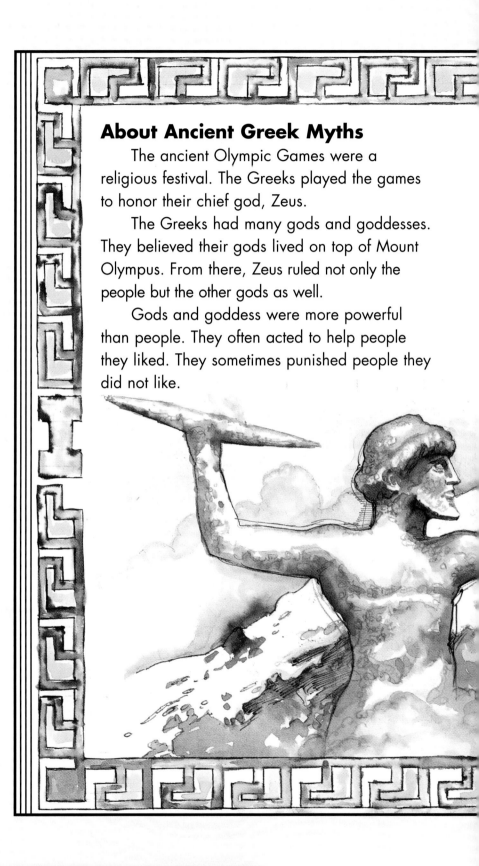

About Ancient Greek Myths

The ancient Olympic Games were a religious festival. The Greeks played the games to honor their chief god, Zeus.

The Greeks had many gods and goddesses. They believed their gods lived on top of Mount Olympus. From there, Zeus ruled not only the people but the other gods as well.

Gods and goddess were more powerful than people. They often acted to help people they liked. They sometimes punished people they did not like.

Stories about the gods and goddesses are called myths. Some myths explain why people are the way they are or why the world is the way it is. Myths may tell why the seasons change. They may tell why there are thunderstorms. They may tell why two people love each other.

Aphrodite was the Greek goddess of love and beauty. She could use her power to help people love each other. As you read the myth about a girl named Atalanta, you will find out how Aphrodite could do this.

Language Tip
Idiom
Atalanta *knew her own mind.* This means that she knew what was important to her.

Reader's Tip
Stop and Think
Do you think Atalanta was like most other young women? Why or why not?

Atalanta loved to run. She was happiest when she was running. She was the fastest runner anyone had ever seen.

Atalanta was a young woman who knew her own mind. She hated to be inside away from the sun and the wind. She did not like to cook or clean.

"I shall never get married," she promised herself. "I could not be myself. I would have to stay inside and cook and clean."

But Atalanta had a problem. Young men saw her running, and they fell in love with her. She did not know how beautiful she was as she raced by.

The young men followed Atalanta around. Each one asked her to marry him. Atalanta refused, but the young men still kept asking.

Language Tip
Vocabulary
Refuse means to say no.

Reader's Tip
Look for Clues
What was Atalanta's plan? Why did she think it would work?

Finally, Atalanta had a plan. She told the young men, "I will marry the man who can win a race with me. If you win the race, I will marry you. But beware," she added. "If I win the race, you will die."

Atalanta hoped that the young men would go away. "I can beat any of them in a race," she thought to herself. "Surely no one will want to race me. If they race me, they know they will die."

She was wrong. Several young men chose to race her. Atalanta ran faster. She won all the races, and all those young men died.

A young athlete, Hippomenes, heard the news of the races. "How could anyone be willing to die for such a stupid dare?" he wondered. "I must go and see for myself."

When he saw Atalanta running as fast and free as the wind, he changed his mind. "I am going to marry her," he promised himself.

Strategy Tip
Understand Plot
Atalanta made a promise to herself. Hippomenes made a promise to himself. What were their promises?

Language Tip
Vocabulary
A *stride* is the length
of a step from one foot
to the other.

Reader's Tip
Make Inferences
Why do you think
Hippomenes took
running lessons from
Atalanta?

Hippomenes asked Atalanta to give him running
lessons. She liked the looks of the young man. She
decided to help him. "I run every morning at seven
o'clock," she said. "If you want to run with me, I will
teach you."

So Atalanta and Hippomenes ran together every
day. She showed him how to use his arms. She showed
him how to make his stride longer. They were a
beautiful sight running together in the early morning
sun. Atalanta liked Hippomenes very much.

One day Hippomenes told Atalanta that he wanted to marry her. He asked to race with her. Atalanta was very sad. She liked Hippomenes, but she knew she could run faster. She wished that he would win the race.

Then she remembered that she had promised never to get married. She had to do her best to win. Sadly she agreed to race him the next day.

Study Tip
Find the Conflict
A conflict happens when two things do not go together. Characters can have conflicts because they want something that does not fit with another thing they want. Atalanta has a conflict. What is it?

Hippomenes was worried. He knew Atalanta was a faster runner. He prayed to Aphrodite, the goddess of love. "You made me love her. Help me to win the race." Aphrodite heard him. She liked Hippomenes. She was angry at Atalanta for refusing to get married.

Aphrodite took Hippomenes to a magic place. There he saw a beautiful tree with yellow leaves and shining golden apples. Aphrodite picked three apples from the tree. She gave them to Hippomenes. "I will tell you what to do with them," she said. She whispered to him how to use the apples.

Strategy Tip
Predict
How do you think the three golden apples will help Hippomenes?

The next day a crowd gathered to watch the race. Atalanta and Hippomenes lined up at the starting line. "Ready, steady, go!" said the starter. Off they went.

At first Hippomenes and Atalanta ran side by side. They were both running as fast as wind. Atalanta began to pull ahead. Hippomenes reached inside his tunic and pulled out a golden apple. He threw it in front of Atalanta. Atalanta saw the beautiful apple. She stopped to pick it up. Hippomenes passed her.

Reader's Tip
Make Inferences
Why do you think Atalanta was interested in the golden apples?

Before long, Atalanta caught up with him. Again she began to pull ahead. Hippomenes threw the second golden apple. Again he passed her as she stopped to pick it up.

The race went on. Hippomenes was getting tired. As Atalanta pulled ahead, he threw the third golden apple off to the side of the race track.

Would Atalanta run off the track to get the third apple? Hippomenes knew he could only win if she went to pick up the apple. Atalanta thought she could get the third apple and still catch up to Hippomenes. She ran off to get the apple.

In the blink of an eye, she was back running on the track. Hippomenes put on a last burst of speed. Gasping for breath, he reached the finish line just before Atalanta. He had won the race!

Atalanta stopped at the finish line and smiled. It was the first time she was happy to lose a race.

Reader's Tip
Understand Character
How did Atalanta change since the beginning of the story? Why was she so happy after losing a race?

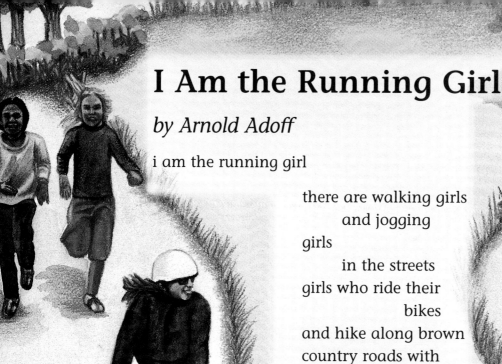

I Am the Running Girl

by Arnold Adoff

i am the running girl

              there are walking girls
                  and jogging
      girls
              in the streets
      girls who ride their
                  bikes
      and hike along brown
      country roads with
                  brothers
      and their friends
      and pull wild flowers
              for their hair
      but

i am the running girl

      there in the moving day
      and i cannot stop to
                  say
      hello

Think About It

How is the girl in the poem like Atalanta?

Sometimes poets do not follow rules for correct writing. In this poem, the poet does not use capital letters or periods.

The poet puts the first line to the left side and the others line to the right side. Why do you think he placed the lines in this way?

Tell what you learned.

1. How are today's Olympic Games different from the ancient games? How are they like the ancient games?

2. What did you learn about the Olympic Games that you did not know before? What would you like to learn more about?

3. What was Hippomenes' problem? How did he resolve it?

What was Atalanta's problem and how did she resolve it?

Oceans

Tell what you know.

Have you ever seen an ocean?

What makes an ocean an ocean?

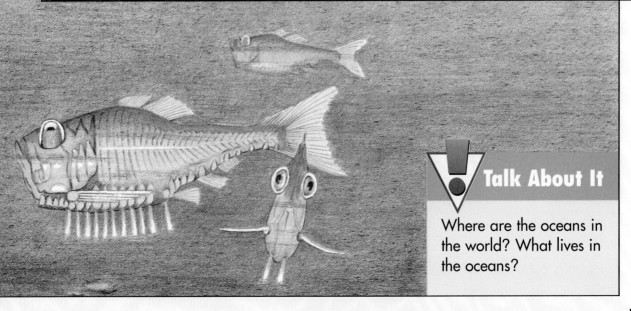

Talk About It

Where are the oceans in the world? What lives in the oceans?

Life Underwater

The Ocean Floor

Look at the map of the ocean floor. How are the ocean floor and dry land alike?

Islands rise above the ocean water. They can be the tops of volcanoes.

Coral reefs are near the shore. The water can be as shallow as 130 feet (40 meters). The temperature of the water is above 65°F (18°C).

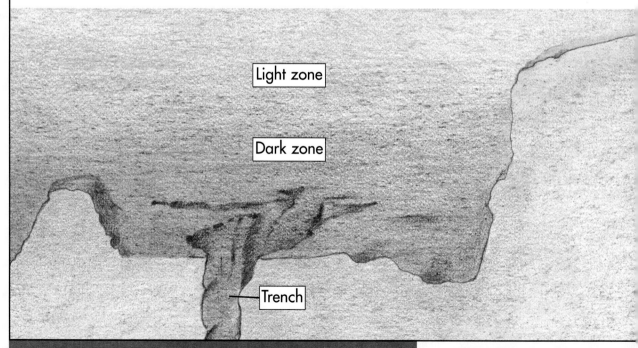

Light zone

Dark zone

Trench

The light zone is at the top of the ocean water. The water can be as deep as 656 feet (200 meters). The temperature of the water is between 65°F and 28°F (18°C and –2°C).

The dark zone is below the light zone. The water can be as deep as 19,700 feet (6,005 meters). The temperature of the water is below 28°F (–2°C).

The trenches are the deepest part of the ocean. The Mariana Trench in the Pacific Ocean is the deepest place in all the earth's oceans. It is about 35,000 feet deep or almost seven miles deep (10,668 meters).

Word Bank

colder

darker

lighter

warmer

more food

less food

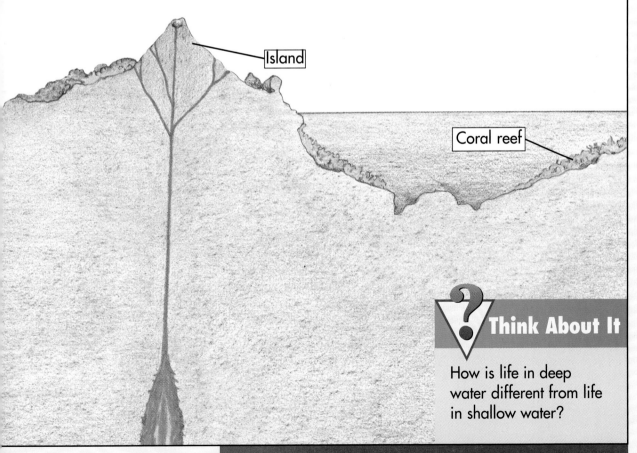

Island

Coral reef

Think About It

How is life in deep water different from life in shallow water?

Coral Reefs, Light Zones, and Dark Zones

Different kinds of animals live at different depths of the ocean. What are some differences among animals at different levels of the ocean?

Coral reefs are in warm water. The shallow water gets lots of sunlight. As many as 5,000 kinds of colorful fish live around coral reefs.

The fish in the light zone have smooth bodies and large fins so they can swim fast. They need to swim fast to catch other fish or to escape their enemies. Fish in the light zones can feed on the many plants in the zone. Plants in the light zone get light from the sun to make the food they need.

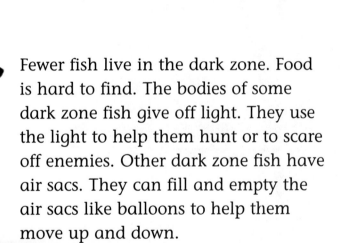

Fewer fish live in the dark zone. Food is hard to find. The bodies of some dark zone fish give off light. They use the light to help them hunt or to scare off enemies. Other dark zone fish have air sacs. They can fill and empty the air sacs like balloons to help them move up and down.

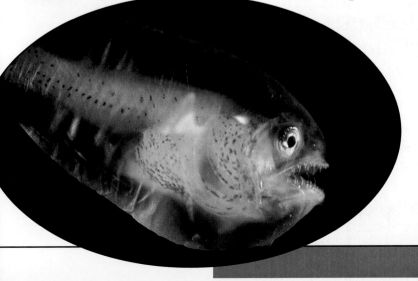

Write About It

Make a chart with the three areas of the ocean. Write about each area.

Why do things float?

Hold an egg and a stone of about the same size. The stone is heavier than the egg because it is denser. Density is how heavy something is for its size.

Things float if their density is less than the density of the water. Salt water is denser than fresh water. Do you think it's easier or harder to float in salt water? Try this to find out.

Things You Need

- jar of water
- salt
- egg
- tablespoon

Follow these steps.

1. Use a tablespoon to place an egg into a jar of water.

2. Remove the egg from the water.

3. Add 2 to 3 tablespoons of salt to the water.

4. Stir the water until the salt dissolves.

5. Use the tablespoon to place the egg into the jar.

1. When I put an egg into fresh water,

2. When I put an egg into salty water,

Talk About It

An egg sinks to the bottom of the water. Which is denser, the egg or the water?

An egg floats in water. Which is denser, the egg or the water?

Oceans of the World

The earth's surface is 71% water and 29% land. Most of the earth's water is in the oceans.

Name the earth's oceans.

NORTH
AMERICA

ATLANTIC OCEAN

PACIFIC OCEAN

The Pacific Ocean is the largest ocean. It covers about 70 million square miles (181 million square kilometers) of the earth's surface. Which continents surround the Pacific Ocean?

SOUTH
AMERICA

ATLANTIC
OCEAN

The Atlantic Ocean is the second largest ocean. It covers about 36 million square miles (93 million square kilometers) of the earth's surface. The Atlantic Ocean is surrounded by North America, South America, Africa, Europe, and Antarctica.

The Arctic Ocean is the smallest ocean. It covers about 5,440,000 square miles (14,090,000 square kilometers) of the earth's surface. The Arctic Ocean is surrounded by North America, Europe, and Asia.

ARCTIC OCEAN

EUROPE

ASIA

AFRICA

PACIFIC OCEAN

INDIAN OCEAN

The Indian Ocean is the third largest ocean. It covers about 29 million square miles (75 million square kilometers) of the earth's surface. Which continents surround the Indian Ocean?

AUSTRALIA

ANTARCTICA

Talk About It

Have you swum in an ocean? Have you crossed an ocean? Tell something about what you did.

Why the Sea Is Salty

Retold by Gail Sakurai

Reader's Tip
This folk tale is from Japan.

Language Tip
Vocabulary
Look at the words that tell about Ichiro and Jiro. Poor is the opposite of wealthy. Greedy is the opposite of generous. Mean-spirited is the opposite of kind-hearted.

Strategy Tip
Understand Plot
The words that tell about Ichiro and Jiro are opposites. The brothers are not alike. This is important in what will happen in the story.

A long time ago in Japan, there lived two brothers. Ichiro, the older brother, was wealthy, greedy, and mean-spirited. Jiro, the younger brother, was poor, generous, and kind-hearted.

It had been a hard winter for Jiro. Now the new year was approaching, and poor Jiro did not have any food to feed his family. He hated to ask his stingy older brother for help, but Jiro couldn't let his wife and children go hungry. Reluctantly, he went off to Ichiro's house.

Language Tip
Vocabulary
A stingy person does not like to share things or spend money.

Language Tip
Vocabulary
Jiro went reluctantly to his brother's house. Jiro did not want to go to his brother's house.

Strategy Tip
Understand Characters
Why do you think Jiro went reluctantly to see his brother?

"You again?" Ichiro shouted as soon as Jiro appeared at his door. "What do you want this time?"

"Please, brother, if it wouldn't trouble you too much, could you spare a little rice so my wife and children will have something to eat?"

"Not a single grain, you worthless dolt! Get out and don't come back!" Ichiro shouted.

Jiro trudged away, wondering how he was going to feed his family. Soon he came upon an old man with a bundle of firewood strapped to his back. The old fellow was stooped over from the weight of his load.

"Good day to you, sir," Jiro greeted the man. "Let me help you with that." Jiro shouldered the heavy bundle and carried it to the old man's home.

Language Tip
Vocabulary
Trudge means "to walk slowly."

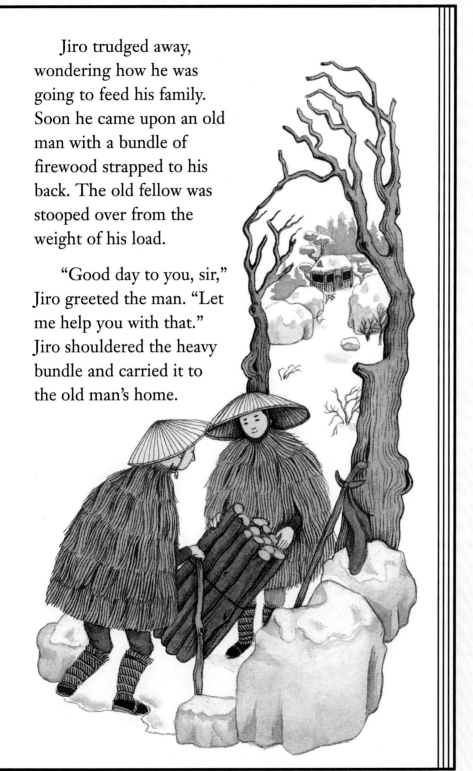

A mortar is a strong bowl. People use it to crush or grind things like rice or medicines into small pieces. It usually comes with a crushing tool called a pestle.

"You seem a worthy young fellow," said the old man. "Please take this as a reward for your kindness." He handed Jiro a small stone mortar, the type used for grinding rice.

"This is a magic mortar," the old fellow explained. "It will give you anything you ask for. All you have to do is turn the handle to the right and say what you want. To stop the mortar, just turn the handle to the left. Remember now—right to start and left to stop."

As soon as Jiro got home, he tried the mortar. Turning the handle to the right, he said, "Rice, please. I'd like some rice."

Rice poured out of the mortar. Soon rice covered the table and flowed onto the floor. "Whoa, stop! That's enough!" Jiro shouted.

Still the rice poured out. Finally, he remembered what the old man had said, and Jiro turned the handle to the left. The rice stopped.

"It really is magic!" cried Jiro, delighted with his good fortune.

Next he asked for *manju*. Barley buns filled with sweet bean paste poured out of the mortar until Jiro turned the handle to the left. "I can have anything I ask for," Jiro realized. "I'll be rich."

Then Jiro asked the mortar for a fine house, a horse, and a stable for the horse. In no time at all, he was the wealthiest man in the village. But he never forgot what it was like to be poor, and every day he handed out rice and manju to the villagers.

When Ichiro learned of his brother's good fortune, he was jealous. He crept up to Jiro's house and peered in the window. He watched Jiro turn the handle of the mortar to the right and ask for manju. Barley buns poured out.

"So that's how he did it," Ichiro said to himself. "It is not fair that the younger brother should have such a treasure. I am the oldest in the family—that mortar should belong to me."

Language Tip
Vocabulary
Peered means "looked."

Strategy Tip
Predict
What do you think Ichiro will do?

Late that night, Ichiro slipped into his brother's house and stole the mortar. On his way out, he spied a stack of manju Jiro had prepared for the next day. He took several buns and placed them in his sack along with the mortar.

Ichiro ran across the fields and over the hills until he reached the sea. He found a small rowboat on the shore. He hopped into the boat and paddled away. Farther and farther out to sea he rowed. "I'll sail all the way to China. They can never catch me there," he decided.

All the rowing made Ichiro hungry. So he took out the buns and began to eat. "These manju are too sweet. They need salt. I wish I had some salt," Ichiro complained. "Ho, what am I saying? I can have anything I want—I have the magic mortar."

Ichiro pulled out the mortar and turned the handle to the right.

"Salt! Salt! Give me salt!" he said.

Salt poured out of the mortar.

"Stop! That's enough!"

Still the salt streamed into the small boat.

"I said STOP! That's enough salt! I don't need anymore!"

Language Tip
Vocabulary
Streamed means that salt flowed out quickly.

But still the salt flowed out in an unending stream. Soon the entire boat was filled with salt. Salt covered Ichiro up to his neck. Just as Ichiro screamed "STOP!" one last time, the boat sank from the weight of all the salt.

Down went the boat to the bottom of the sea. Down went Ichiro, and down went the mortar. The mortar came to rest on the sea bed, where it remains to this day still grinding salt.

Language Tip
Vocabulary
The sea bed is the same as the ocean floor.

Study Tip
Folk Tales
Folk tales are stories that people have told for many years. Some folk tales tell about how something in the world began. At the end of many folk tales, good things happen to good people, and bad things happen to bad people. Why is this story a good example of a folk tale?

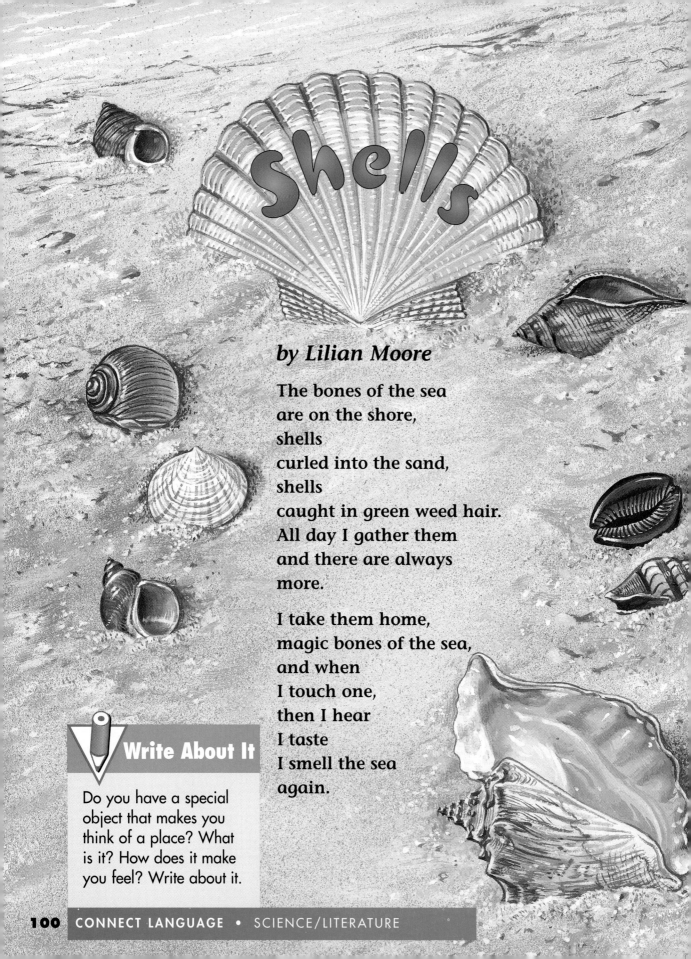

Shells

by Lilian Moore

The bones of the sea
are on the shore,
shells
curled into the sand,
shells
caught in green weed hair.
All day I gather them
and there are always
more.

I take them home,
magic bones of the sea,
and when
I touch one,
then I hear
I taste
I smell the sea
again.

Write About It

Do you have a special
object that makes you
think of a place? What
is it? How does it make
you feel? Write about it.

Tell what you learned.

CHAPTER 5

1. Describe the ocean. Tell about the zones and the animals.

2. Make a word web about ocean life.

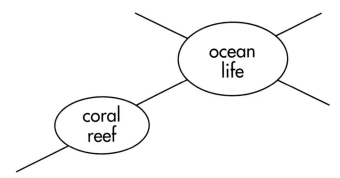

3. What lesson does the story "Why the Sea Is Salty" teach?

Taking Care of the Oceans

Tell what you know.

How do people use the oceans?

Hawaii

MISS DIANE
STONINGTON, MAINE.

Talk About It

Why are oceans important? How can people take care of the oceans?

How do people pollute the oceans?

People **pollute** the oceans by throwing garbage on the beach or into the water. Garbage harms plants and animals in the oceans.

Factories pollute the oceans by dumping chemicals into the water. Like garbage, chemicals harm plants and animals.

Farmers pollute the oceans by using chemicals to kill insects. Farmers also pollute the oceans by using chemical fertilizers to help make plants grow. The chemicals get into waterways and run into the ocean. The chemicals help farmers, but they harm ocean animals and plants.

Accidents also cause pollution. Oil tankers can pollute the ocean by spilling oil into the water. The oil can kill fish and birds. It can also kill the tiny plants and animals in the ocean that are food for larger animals.

Talk About It

What are the causes of pollution? What are the effects of pollution?

Why do people pollute the oceans?

Some Pollution Solutions

Governments, farmers, factories, and scientists can all help reduce pollution.

Governments can pass laws to control pollution. Governments can make factories pay money in fines for polluting water.

Farmers can stop using dangerous chemicals. Farmers can use other insects like lady bugs to eat harmful insects. Farmers can use chemicals that are less harmful to plants and animals.

Factories can stop dumping dangerous chemicals into the water. When they finish using harmful chemicals, they can store them in special places.

Not all chemicals pollute. Scientists can find safe chemicals that do not harm plants and animals. Then factories and farmers can stop using harmful chemicals.

CAUTION

RADIOACTIVE MATERIALS

Write About It

Find pictures in magazines or newspapers that show people polluting the environment or protecting the environment. Write about one of them.

What can you do to help the environment?

Everyone can help take care of the environment. Garbage pollutes the oceans and the land. Everyone can make less garbage. Here are some things you can do.

Reduce

Use less paper. When you write, use both sides of every sheet of paper. When you work in the kitchen, clean up with cloth rags, not with paper towels. This makes less garbage.

Reuse

Think of the things you use once and throw away. When you drink from a plastic cup, don't throw it away. Wash it and use it again.

Think of other uses for plastic things. For example, you can plant seeds in plastic bottles. When you reuse things, you make less garbage.

Recycle

Materials like plastic and newspaper can be recycled. Plastic containers can be recycled to make new plastic containers. Newspapers can be recycled to make new paper. When materials are recycled, there is less garbage.

Try It Out

Plan a Reuse It Day. Bring in plastics and newspapers from home. How many different ways can you think of to use these things? Make something that reuses what you brought.

Farming the Water

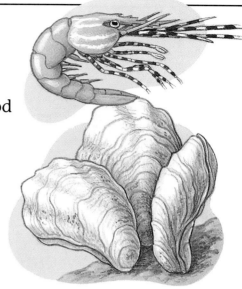

Growing plants and animals on land for food is called agriculture. Raising plants and animals in the water is called aquaculture.

Fish are an important source of food. The number of fish in the ocean is getting smaller. So people are farming fish.

Fish farming is raising baby fish until they grow into large adult fish. Then the fish are taken to market. They are bought and eaten.

On fish farms in the oceans, fish grow in large nets or cages. Ocean farms are usually in the shallow waters near the shore.

Fish farming is not new. The Chinese have been farming fish for thousands of years. In Japan, people have raised shellfish like oysters and shrimp for many years.

Each year fish farms now raise about 11 million tons (10 million metric tons) of fish. This number will get bigger and bigger.

Word Bank

boat

ground

plow

rain

seed

temperature

tractor

? Think About It

How is agriculture like aquaculture? How is it different?

NEIGHBORHOOD NEWS

A Day at the Beach for Sixth-Graders

Sixth-graders from four local schools joined together last Saturday to clean up the beaches at Ocean Haven. The students divided into small groups to pick up garbage before it could wash into the ocean. They collected more than forty bags of trash during the day.

Summer tourists had left large amounts of garbage on the beach. It was littered with bottles, cans, and pieces of plastic.

"We wanted to clean our beach because we learned how garbage can harm animals," said Brian Sanders, 11, from Lincoln School.

▲ Students from local schools clean up beach.

The students had learned that large pieces of plastic in the ocean can trap animals like a net. Holders for six-packs of soda can get around sea birds' necks. The birds are not able to breathe and they die.

Veronica Brown, 12, from Hawthorne School said, "It was exciting to work together and show we care about the ocean."

Talk About It

Newspaper articles answer five questions. Find the answers to these questions: who? what? when? where? why?

Yellow Submarine

by John Lennon and
Paul McCartney

In the town where I was born
lived a man who sailed to sea.
And he told us of his life
in the land of submarines.
So we sailed up to the sun
till we found the sea of green.
And we lived beneath the waves
in our yellow submarine.
We all live in a yellow submarine,
yellow submarine, yellow submarine.
We all live in a yellow submarine,
yellow submarine, yellow submarine.

Tell what you learned.

1. Why is the ocean important to people?

2. What are some causes of ocean pollution? What are some of the effects of ocean pollution? Make a chart.

Causes of Pollution	Effects of Pollution
Oil tankers spill oil in the ocean.	Sea birds are covered in oil and die.

3. Imagine you are the leader of a group of students who want to help protect the environment. Think of a project that the group could do in your community. Write a newspaper advertisement for the event.

The Ancient Romans

Tell what you know.

These are some things from ancient Rome. What do these things tell about the ancient Romans?

Talk About It

If you were able to travel back through time to ancient Rome, what would you find?

Do you find any of these things in a city today?

117

CHAPTER 7

The Roman Empire

The Growth of Rome

The city of Rome began about 2,700 years ago. The first Romans farmed and took care of sheep and goats. From these small beginnings, the Romans built a great **empire.** They built a strong army that conquered all the land and people around the Mediterranean Sea. When the Romans were most powerful, about A.D. 96–180, they controlled most of Europe, including part of England.

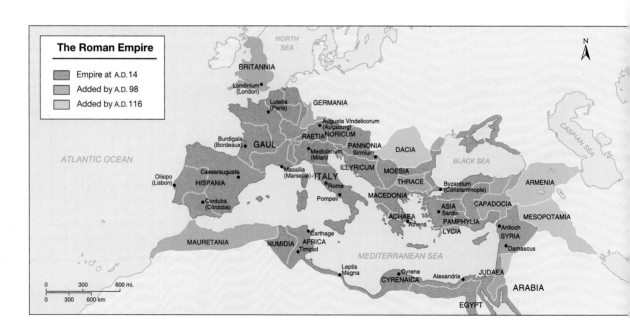

The Roman Empire

- Empire at A.D. 14
- Added by A.D. 98
- Added by A.D. 116

The Romans did more than win battles. They learned from the people they conquered. For example, they borrowed the idea of using coins for trade and commerce from the ancient Greeks. They even used the Greek gods, but they changed the gods' names.

The Romans also brought things and ideas to the people they conquered. They brought laws and government. They brought cities and buildings. They brought their language. These things lasted long after the Roman Empire itself had ended.

? Think About It

What things would you like to borrow from the country you came from?

The Romans were builders.

The Romans were good builders. Some of the things they built can still be seen today.

As the Roman Empire grew, the Romans built roads to connect the parts of their empire with Rome. Roman armies could move quickly throughout the empire on these roads.

The roads were well built. First, workers dug a ditch and filled it with stones. On top of this, they put stones that were cut to fit together closely. Many of these roads can still be seen today.

Romans also built tall structures called **aqueducts.** Aqueducts brought water into cities from places outside the cities. The water flowed in channels above tall arches. A few of these aqueducts still stand today.

The Romans also built huge **arenas** throughout their empire. People went to these for entertainment. Fights between people and animals were popular. The large arena in Rome, called the Colosseum, held 50,000 people. People today still go to some of these arenas, to see sports events and musical performances.

Channel with water

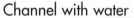

Arch

Talk About It

Are there any old buildings near your school? What do they tell about the people who built them?

Should people save old things? Why?

What was Roman law?

Early in their history, the Romans formed a republic. In a republic, **citizens** can vote. They can choose their rulers.

At first, only rich men were citizens. Then poor men demanded the right to vote. The poor men refused to serve in the army. Finally, the rulers let the poor men vote too. But women were never allowed to vote.

Poor people still felt that the law was not equal for all. So the rulers of Rome carved the laws in stone. These written laws came to be known as the Twelve Tables of Law. They were put in the forum, the center of town and of the government. Here everyone could read the laws.

It was an important step to have laws in writing. Now the law was the same for everyone, for rich people and poor people.

The stone tablets were destroyed during an attack on Rome, but the thinking behind them spread through the Roman Empire. Many nations copied the ideas of Roman law.

Write About It

Make a list of "laws" that everyone in your class follows. How do these laws help you and your classmates?

Latin Words in English

Latin was the language of the ancient Romans. It was spoken all over their empire. Latin is no longer spoken, but the Spanish, French, and Italian languages come from Latin.

Some English words are made from parts of Latin words. A few of these are in the chart.

Latin Word Part	Meaning of the Latin Word Part	English Word
ped	foot	pedestrian, pedal
aqua	water	aquarium
vid	see	videotape

▲ A *pedestrian* goes places on foot. People on bicycles use their feet to push *pedals*.

▲ You need to change the water in your pet fish's *aquarium*.

▲ You can see a *videotape* on your TV.

▲ This is Martha's room.

▲ Martha rearranged the furniture in her room.

Some English **prefixes** also come from Latin. A prefix is added to the beginning of a word. It adds to the word's meaning. For example, *re-* means "again." The word *arrange* means "to put in order." *Rearrange* means "to put in order again."

▲ Then she rearranged it once more.

Latin Prefix	Meaning	Example of English Word
pre-	before	pregame ("before the game")
re-	again	rewrite ("write again")
uni-	one	unicycle ("a bike with one wheel")

Think About It

What is the Latin word part in *aquaculture?* What do you think an aquatic animal is?

Are there any words from your native language used in English? What are they?

Does your native language use any words from English? What are they?

Roman Recipes

Romans liked to eat good food. These two dishes could have been the appetizer and the dessert at a Roman banquet. Try these foods that the Romans ate.

Salad with Eggs and Tuna

Ingredients

half of a head of lettuce
one can of tuna fish
three sliced hard-boiled eggs
oil and vinegar salad dressing
two tablespoons of anchovy or fish paste

Directions

Break the lettuce into small pieces and place it in a bowl. Drain the tuna. Use a fork to break it into small pieces. Mix some fish paste with the salad dressing. Toss the tuna, lettuce, and salad dressing. Place the eggs on top.

Stuffed Dates

Ingredients

24 pitted dates (seeds are already removed)

24 chopped nuts (cashews or walnuts)

one tablespoon of salt

one half cup of warm honey

Directions

Place the jar of honey in a pan of hot water from the faucet to warm. Fill the insides of the dates with the nuts. Roll the dates in salt.

Dip them in the warm honey, and eat them.

Make a mosaic.

The ancient Romans decorated their homes with mosaics. Mosaics are pictures made with small pieces of stone or glass.

Make your own mosaic.

Things You Need

 a large piece of cardboard

 a pencil

 glue

scissors

small pieces of colored paper or colored peas and beans

---

1. Draw a picture or a pattern on the cardboard. Draw in lines for different colors you want to use.

2. Put some glue on a small area of your drawing. Paste the pieces of paper or the beans onto that area. Repeat this step until your mosaic is filled in.

Tell what you learned.

1. How are the buildings of the ancient Romans like the buildings in a city today?

2. Why were the ancient Romans important?

3. English has borrowed Latin words and word parts. Give some examples of these.

4. What was the most interesting thing you learned about the ancient Romans?

Volcanoes in History

Word Bank

explosion

fire

lightning

smoke

Tell what you know.

What are volcanoes?

What do the pictures show about volcanoes?

Talk About It

Would you live near a volcano? Why or why not?

Have you ever seen a volcano? What was it like?

A volcano erupts in A.D. 79.

Pompeii was a city near Mount Vesuvius. The people who lived there in A.D. 79 did not know that Vesuvius was a volcano. It had been quiet for about 1,200 years.

But Mount Vesuvius was going to **erupt.** When a volcano erupts, hot rock from deep under the earth bursts out. Hot liquid rock called **lava** often flows out of the volcano. Very tiny pieces of rock called **ash** may fill the air. Larger pieces of rock may also blow out.

▼ Mt. Vesuvius erupting in 1944

In August of A.D. 79, strange things began to happen at Pompeii. The earth shook. Animals became frightened. Water in wells dried up.

Then, on August 24, the top of Mount Vesuvius blew off. A huge cloud of ash came out of the volcano. Hot rocks fell from the sky. People tried to escape, but many were killed by the ash and the poison gas in the air. About 2,000 people died in Pompeii.

Twelve feet (four meters) of ash and rocks covered Pompeii. The town was forgotten until the 1700s. Then people began to dig it out.

Word Bank

earthquake

flood

hurricane

storm

Talk About It

Volcanoes are just one natural disaster. What other natural disasters are there? What can people do to predict and prevent such disasters?

Vesuvius preserves the past.

When archaeologists dug out Pompeii and nearby places, they learned a great deal about the life of the ancient Romans. They found places just as they were when the volcano erupted in A.D. 79.

Pompeii's streets were made of stone. Some ▶ were narrow. There was only room for a donkey with baskets. Others were as wide as 23 feet (7 meters). Vehicles such as carts and chariots went down them.

Houses in ancient Rome ▶ often had a square garden in the center. This was called an atrium. The rooms were built on the four sides of the square.

The forum was the center ▶ of town life. The government buildings were in this part of Pompeii. There was a law court. There was also a market. The most splendid buildings around the forum were temples to the gods. One was the temple of Jupiter, the king of the gods.

▲ This large outdoor theater in Pompeii had seats for 5,000 people. People went to see plays here. The actors in ancient times were as well-known as movie stars today. Games in which animals were killed took place in a larger theater outside of Pompeii.

Try It Out

Make a record of a day in the life of your school. Take pictures. Label them and make a photo essay.

▲ This picture shows the back of a bakery. The Romans used millstones like these to make flour for bread. The millstones ground grain into flour. The grain was poured into the top of the millstone. Donkeys often turned the millstones.

▲ The loaf of bread is from Pompeii. It is now as hard as rock. Round loaves of bread like these are still made in Italian bakeries.

This shop was a snack ▶ bar. People could eat while they stood up in the shop or they could take food out. This shop probably sold hot and cold drinks as well as snacks.

This is a kitchen set up to prepare a meal on the day the volcano erupted. Slaves would prepare food for the family using these pots and pans. ▼

▲ Glasses and dishes like these were widely used in rich people's homes.

Write About It

What things that you see in the pictures are like things people use today? What things are different?

What is a volcano?

Volcanoes are openings in the earth's surface. Hot rock from deep under the earth bursts out, or erupts. The eruptions cause mountains to form. The hot liquid rock that comes out of a volcano is called lava. Pieces of rock also may come out of a volcano.

There are three kinds of volcanoes:

▲ Paricutín in Mexico is a cinder cone volcano.

1. Shield volcanoes form when lava slowly flows through several openings in the earth. Over the years, the lava forms a low mountain. When a shield volcano erupts, there is not a big explosion.

2. Cinder cone volcanoes form when rocks shoot out of an opening in the earth. The rocks fall back to earth as cinders or small pieces of burned rock. The cinders form a cone-shaped mountain.

Mount Kilauea in Hawaii is a shield volcano. ▶

3. Composite volcanoes are a mixture of the two other kinds. They form when eruptions of lava and cinders pile up to make high mountains. Some composite volcanoes have violent eruptions. Mount Vesuvius is a composite volcano.

Mount Fuji in Japan is a ▶ composite volcano.

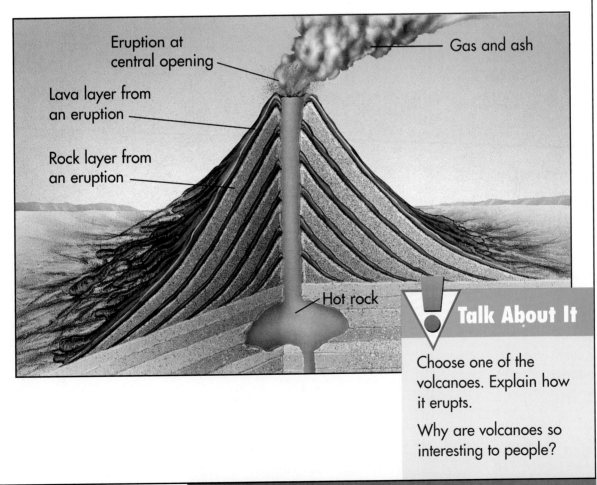

Eruption at central opening

Gas and ash

Lava layer from an eruption

Rock layer from an eruption

Hot rock

Talk About It

Choose one of the volcanoes. Explain how it erupts.

Why are volcanoes so interesting to people?

An Ancient Roman Myth: The God Vulcan

Like the ancient Greeks, the ancient Romans believed in gods and goddesses. Gods made good things and bad things happen to humans. Stories about the gods and what they did are called myths.

Reader's Tip
In Roman myths, the god Jupiter and his wife Juno were often fighting with each other.

Of all the gods and goddesses, Vulcan was the only one who was born ugly. He was the son of the most important and powerful of the Roman gods, Jupiter and Juno.

Vulcan lived on Mount Olympus with the other gods and goddesses. But then one time he took his mother's side in an argument with Jupiter. In a fit of anger, Jupiter threw Vulcan from Mount Olympus. After the fall, Vulcan was lame as well as ugly. And he no longer lived with the other gods.

Vulcan was an expert at metalworking. He used fire to heat metal. Then he hammered the metal into tools for farmers or weapons for soldiers. When he hammered, sparks flew. Vulcan liked to work inside mountains. There no one would bother him.

Language Tip
Vocabulary
Lame means "not being able to walk well because a person has an injured leg or foot."

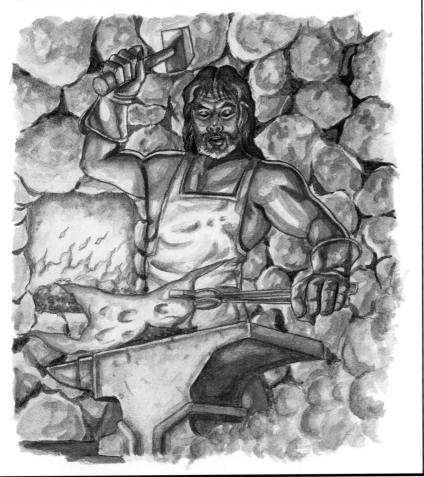

After a while, Jupiter decided to use Vulcan's skill. He wanted Vulcan to make thunderbolts of metal. Jupiter wanted to use the thunderbolts as a warning. They would let people know when he was unhappy with what they were doing. Vulcan agreed to make the thunderbolts. After all, Jupiter was the most powerful god.

Vulcan worked hard. Sparks flew out of his mountain day and night. The thunderbolts that Vulcan made were very beautiful and very frightening. Jupiter was quite pleased with them. After that, Vulcan was again welcome at Mount Olympus.

But Vulcan kept on doing his beautiful metal work. He was happiest when he was inside a mountain working over a fire.

When people saw a mountain explode with smoke, sparks, and hot lava, they thought Vulcan was inside the mountain working. So they called mountains that threw out fire volcanoes after Vulcan, the god of fire.

Strategy Tip
Stop and Think
This myth tells the origin of two things in nature. What are they?

Hill of Fire

*by Thomas
P. Lewis*

Reader's Tip
This story takes place in
Mexico. When the story
begins, a young boy,
Pablo, is helping his
father to plow the
family's cornfield.

The ox pulled, and the plow turned up the soil.
Suddenly the plow stopped. The farmer and his son
pushed, and the ox pulled, but the plow did not
move. It sank into the earth. It went down, down,
down into a little hole.

The little hole became a bigger hole. There was a
noise deep under the ground, as if something big had
growled.

The farmer looked. Pablo looked. The ox turned its head. White smoke came from the hole in the ground.

"Run!" said the farmer. "Run!"

There was a loud CRACK, and the earth opened wide. The farmer ran, Pablo ran, and the ox ran too. Fire and smoke came from the ground.

The farmer ran all the way to the village. He ran inside the church and rang the old bell.

The other farmers came from their fields. People came out of their houses. "Look!" said the farmer. "Look there!"

Language Tip
Sound Words
Some words in English are sound words. *Crack* means a sound like the one you make when you say the word. As you read on, look for another sound word.

That night no one slept. Everyone watched the fire in the sky. It came from where the farmer's field had been.

There was a loud BOOM, and another, and another. Hot lava came out of the earth. Steaming lava spread over the ground, through the trees. It came toward the farmer's house. It came toward the village. Pieces of burning stone flew in the air.

Strategy Tip
Stop and Think
Why did no one sleep that night?

Strategy Tip
Stop and Think
Use what you learned in
this chapter. What do
you think is happening?
How do you know?

Strategy Tip
Personification
Authors sometimes compare things and animals to people. Here the author says the earth was coughing. Coughing is an action that people do.

Language Tip
Vocabulary
A *burro* is a small donkey.

Study Tip
Use What You Know
As you read any story, use what you know to help understand it better. As you read this story, you can use what you know about volcanoes and volcano eruptions to help you understand what is happening in the story.

The earth was coughing. Every time it coughed, the hill of fire grew bigger. In a few days the hill was as big as a mountain. And every few minutes there was a loud BOOM. Squirrels and rabbits ran, and birds flew away from the fire. People led their burros and their oxen to safety.

Pieces of burning ash flew everywhere. The farmer and his neighbors put wet cloths over their noses to keep out the smoke.

Some of the people went close to the steaming lava. They carried big crosses. They prayed for the fire to stop. The farmer and Pablo watched from the side of a hill.

When the booming stopped and the fires grew smaller, the farmer's house was gone. The school was gone. The market was gone. Half the village was gone.

Strategy Tip
Cause and Effect
In this part of the story, the author is talking about the effects of the volcano. What are they? Find them in the story.

Strategy Tip
Stop and Think
Why do the soldiers laugh? Did the farmer really cause the volcano to erupt and form?

One day some men in uniform came in cars and trucks.

"So you are the one with the plow that opened up the earth," they said to the farmer.

They laughed.

"You are lucky to be alive, *amigo*."

The soldiers looked at the village. "Everyone must go!" the captain said. "It is not safe to live here any longer." The farmer and his wife and Pablo and all the people of the village went with the soldiers. They rode away in the trucks.

The farmer found a new house. It was bigger than the one they lived in before.

It was not far from the old one. But it was far enough away to be safe from *El Monstruo*, which means "The Monster." That is the name the people gave to the great volcano.

Language Tip
Vocabulary
Amigo is the Spanish word for friend.

Reader's Tip
This story is based on a true event. The volcano Paricutín in Mexico began to form in 1943 from a hole in a cornfield. When the volcano stopped erupting in 1952, it was 1,345 feet (410 meters) tall. It is a cinder cone volcano.

V is for Volcano

by William Jay Smith

A bright mountaintop:
It rumbles and grumbles
Until it can't stop
With hot rock and ashes
It then blows its top

Write About It

Make a dictionary with words about the ancient Romans. Write a description for each word. For example, you could start with "A is for aqueduct. An aqueduct carried water to cities."

Tell what you learned.

1. Imagine that you are a reporter for a newspaper in a town near Pompeii. Tell about the volcano blowing up.

2. Pretend you are a tour guide for Pompeii. Make an advertisement for your tour. Draw pictures of the places and artifacts you show. Label the pictures. What do those places and artifacts tell you about the people who lived there?

3. In the story "Hill of Fire," the boy and his father had to move to a new place. Why do you think they chose to stay nearby?

4. Create a city. What would you include?

The Physics of Fun

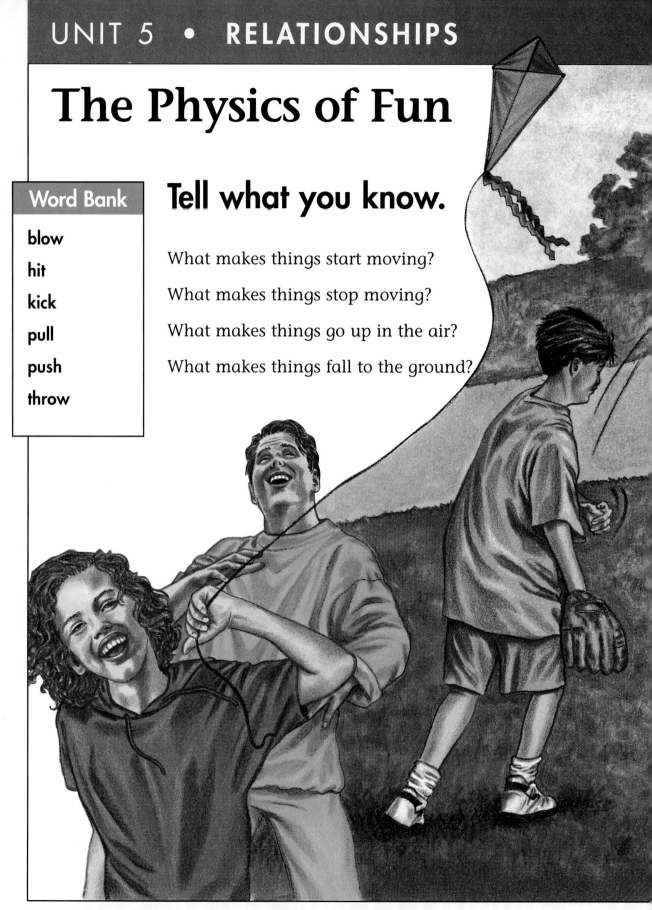

Word Bank

- blow
- hit
- kick
- pull
- push
- throw

Tell what you know.

What makes things start moving?

What makes things stop moving?

What makes things go up in the air?

What makes things fall to the ground?

Talk About It

What is the relationship between how hard you kick a ball and how fast and how far the ball will go?

What makes things move?

Motion

Children run and jump. Animals swim and climb trees. The Earth is moving too. All of this is **motion.**

You start an object in motion by using an outside **force.** A force is a push, pull, or kick that starts something moving. Wind and water are forces too.

When something is in motion, it stays moving until an outside force stops it. When you run down a hill, you can't stop quickly. Your legs keep taking you forward. When you throw a ball, it does not stop exactly where it lands. It rolls on.

Word Bank

eat

jump

run

walk

Talk About It

Tell about some activities you do every day. How do they use motion?

Friction

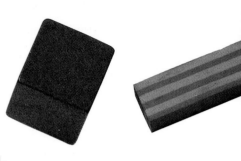

When you kick a ball, it rolls. Then it slows down and stops.

The ball slows down and stops because of **friction.** Friction is a force that comes from one object rubbing against another. As the ball rolls, the ground and the ball rub together. Friction makes the ball stop moving.

A rough surface makes more friction than a smooth surface. Try this experiment to see how friction works.

Things You Need

metal cookie sheet		wooden board
five objects for sliding:	a penny	a flat eraser
a can	a square block	an ice cube

1. Place a metal cookie sheet and a wooden board on a table. Place them so they work as slides.

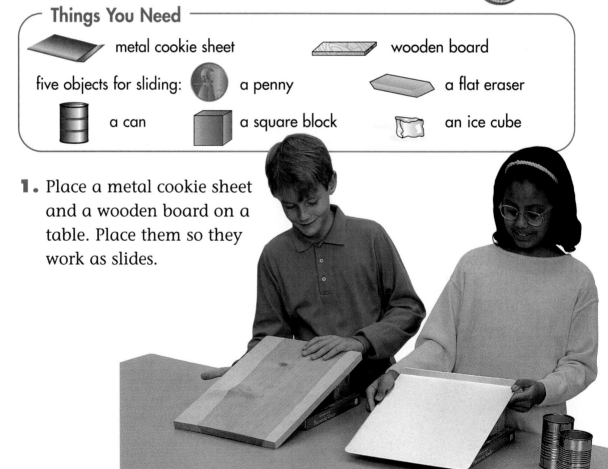

My Record

These are smooth objects:

These are rough objects:

Does the coin move more slowly on wood or on metal?

Try the other objects.

2. See how each object slides down. Which objects move more slowly on the wooden board than on the metal cookie sheet?

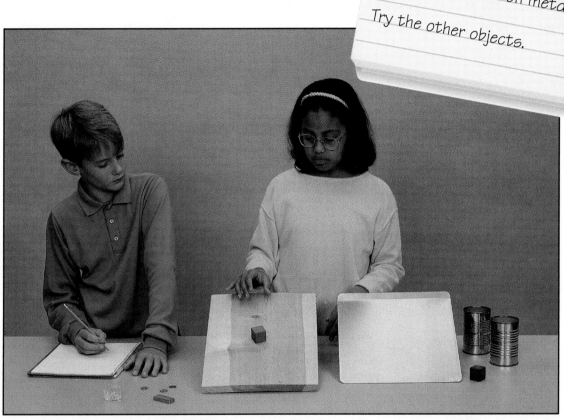

3. Talk about the results in class. Answer these questions: Do rough objects move faster or slower than smooth objects? Do objects move more slowly down the metal cookie sheet or the wooden board? Why?

Write About It

Think of other examples from your everyday life that show friction. Draw pictures of them and label them.

Gravity

When you kick a ball into the air, what brings it back to the ground? One answer is **gravity.** Gravity is a force. It pulls everything down to the ground.

When you walk, you stay on the ground because of gravity. Without gravity, things would float in the air like astronauts in space.

Do heavy things fall faster than light things?
Try this experiment to see how gravity works.

Things You Need

 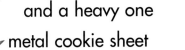 two balls—a light one
and a heavy one

  modeling clay

metal cookie sheet

rolling pin

1. Put a metal cookie sheet on the ground.

2. Hold the two balls the same distance above the cookie sheet.

3. Drop the balls at exactly the same time. Listen carefully. Do the balls fall at the same rate of speed?

4. Roll out the clay on the cookie sheet. Drop the two balls again. What do you see in the clay? Which ball fell with greater force?

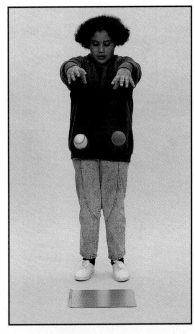

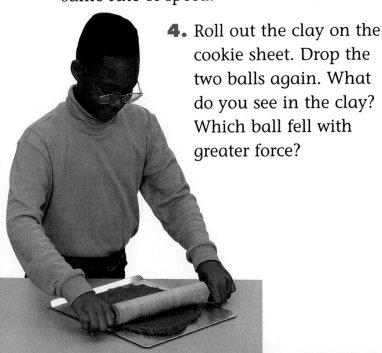

Think About It

Will a feather and a marker fall at the same rate of speed? Make a prediction and try it. Talk about the results.

Can friction and gravity change a marble race?

Friction and gravity slow down moving objects. Try this experiment to see how they slow down marbles. Work with a team.

Things You Need

goggles
wood board
wood strips
white glue
marbles

cardboard tubes
nails
paper clips
rubber bands
stopwatch

1. Get a flat board. It will work as a slide.

2. Use wood strips to make a ramp. Glue the strips to the board. Let the glue dry.

3. Roll a marble down the ramp. Use a stopwatch to time it.

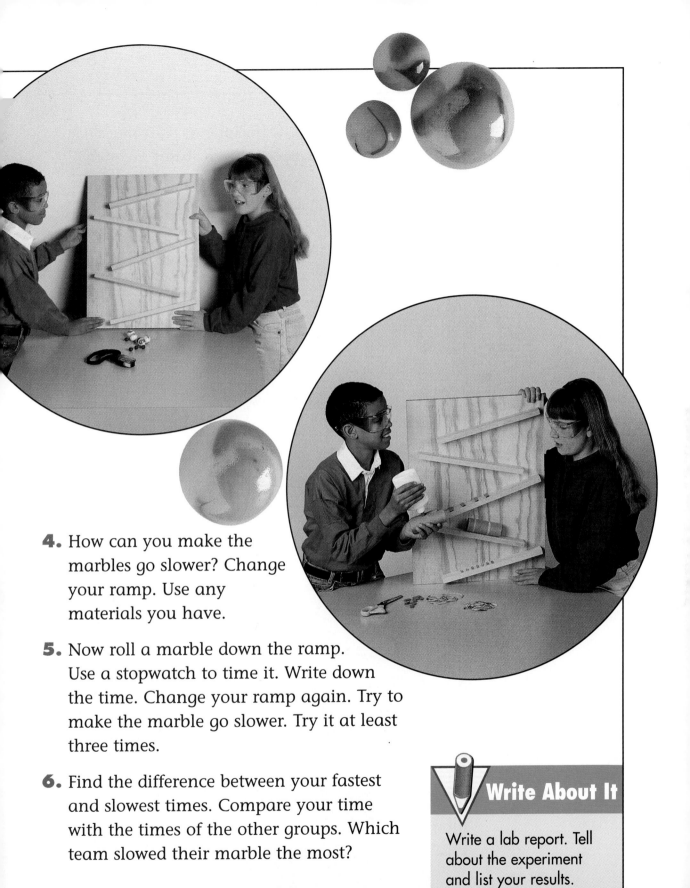

4. How can you make the marbles go slower? Change your ramp. Use any materials you have.

5. Now roll a marble down the ramp. Use a stopwatch to time it. Write down the time. Change your ramp again. Try to make the marble go slower. Try it at least three times.

6. Find the difference between your fastest and slowest times. Compare your time with the times of the other groups. Which team slowed their marble the most?

Write About It

Write a lab report. Tell about the experiment and list your results.

The Tug Of War

by Pleasant DeSpain

Vocabulary Tip
Language
Tug of war is a game of motion. People play it by pulling on both ends of a rope. The winner is the one who can pull the hardest.

ONCE LONG AGO Tortoise was crawling along a jungle trail. He had just been chased out of the river by Hippo and was not in a friendly mood. Suddenly, Elephant rushed across the path and nearly stepped on Tortoise.

"Watch where you're going, you big, lumbering fool!" cried Tortoise.

Elephant did not like to be insulted and replied, "You watch where you're going, tiny Tortoise, and also watch your sharp tongue. It could get you into trouble."

"You don't frighten me," said Tortoise defiantly. "I'm stronger than you realize. In fact, I'm as strong as you."

"No, you're not!" trumpeted Elephant. "You are too small to have my strength, and if you don't apologize for your silly boasts, I'm going to step on you!"

Strategy Tip
Make Inferences
You can use what you know about the story to help you figure out a new word or expression. What does Elephant mean when he says Tortoise has a "sharp tongue"?

Language Tip
Vocabulary
When people talk about how good they are at doing something, they are making a boast.

"I have a better idea," said Tortoise, as he took hold of a stout vine. "I challenge you to a contest of strength, a tug-of-war. You hold one end of this long vine with your trunk and I'll go down to the river with the other end. I will try to pull you into the water and you will try to pull me into the jungle. When I yell, 'Pull, O mighty beast, pull!' the contest begins."

"Very well," agreed Elephant, "it will be fun to make a fool of you."

Tortoise took the other end of the vine and disappeared into the thick jungle growth. When he arrived at the river's edge, he called, "Hippo! Hippo! Stick your head out of the water if you're brave enough!"

The huge hippo slowly surfaced and swam over to Tortoise. "Are you calling me, little one?"

"Yes, big one," answered Tortoise. "You chased me out of the river earlier today, and now I'm mad. You think that you're strong because of your size. I'm going to show you that I, too, am strong."

Strategy Tip
Make Inferences
What does Hippo mean
when he tells Tortoise
that his words are
bigger than his shell?

Strategy Tip
Stop and Think
Why do you think
Tortoise challenges
Hippo?

Hippo was amused by Tortoise's angry speech and said, "Your words are bigger than your shell, little friend. How can you prove such a boast?"

"By challenging you to a tug of war!" said Tortoise. "You take this end of the vine in your mouth and I'll go into the jungle and take up the other end. You try to pull me into the river, and I'll try to pull you out of it. I'll yell, 'Pull, O mighty beast, pull!' when I'm ready."

Hippo laughed and said, "I agree. It will be fun to teach you some manners."

Hippo bit on the end of the vine and Tortoise walked back into the trees. Then he yelled in his loudest voice, "Pull, O mighty beast, pull!"

Both Elephant and Hippo began to pull, and they pulled and pulled with all of their strength, but neither could gain on the other.

Strategy Tip
Understand Vocabulary
Use the other words in the sentence to guess the meaning of *yelled*.

Strategy Tip
Make a Picture
Make a picture in your mind of Elephant and Hippo on page 170 of the story. What makes this part of the story funny?

Language Tip
Vocabulary
A *tie* happens when a game ends and there is no winner. No one loses, but no one wins.

"Tortoise is as strong as Hippo!" thought Elephant as he grunted and pulled even harder.

"Tortoise is as strong as Elephant!" thought Hippo as he strained and pulled harder still.

When he could see that Elephant and Hippo were growing very tired, Tortoise yelled, "Stop, stop! Let's call it a tie. I'm afraid that the vine will break!"

Both of the large beasts were happy to stop pulling.

Tortoise ran to Elephant, and as soon as Elephant caught his breath, he said, "You are strong, friend Tortoise, and I will be careful of where I step from now on."

Then Tortoise went down to the river and Hippo said, "I'm sorry for chasing you out of the water, little friend. You are much too strong to be joked with."

Tortoise was treated with great respect from that time forth.

Study Tip
Trickster Tales
Many folk tales have tricksters. A trickster can be an animal or a person. Tricksters try to fool others. They think they are smart. Who is the trickster in this story? How does the trickster fool the others?

There's Motion Everywhere

by *John Travers Moore*

There's motion everywhere—
On earth, in sea, in sky and air:
Traveling specks and microbes too
have their moment passing through—
All life turns on being new.

Think About It

The author of the poem
writes that there is
motion on earth, in the
sea, and in the air.
What examples can you
give to show that the
author is right?

Tell what you learned.

1. Draw a picture of one way to make an object move. Label your picture.

2. How do gravity and friction work to stop a baseball?

3. Draw a picture of what your classroom might look like if there were no force of gravity.

4. People often are afraid of other people who are a lot bigger than they are. Was Tortoise afraid of Elephant and Hippo? How do you know?

5. Play a tug-of-war game. What forces of motion do you use in a tug of war?

10 Physics of Roller Coasters

Word Bank

exciting

fun

safe

scary

Tell what you know.

What is it like to ride on a roller coaster?

How do you feel as you go up the hills?

How do you feel as you go down the hills?

What do you see? What do you hear?

Talk About It

What do you like best about riding on a roller coaster? What don't you like?

Why do people like roller coasters?

175

How does a roller coaster work?

A roller coaster is fun and scary. First, it goes slowly up, up, up a big hill. Then it zooms and twists down a track.

A roller coaster train needs a motor to climb the first hill. After that, it runs because of the forces of motion.

The train goes down the first hill because of gravity. As it zooms down the hill, it builds up **energy** from the motion. Energy is the ability to do work.

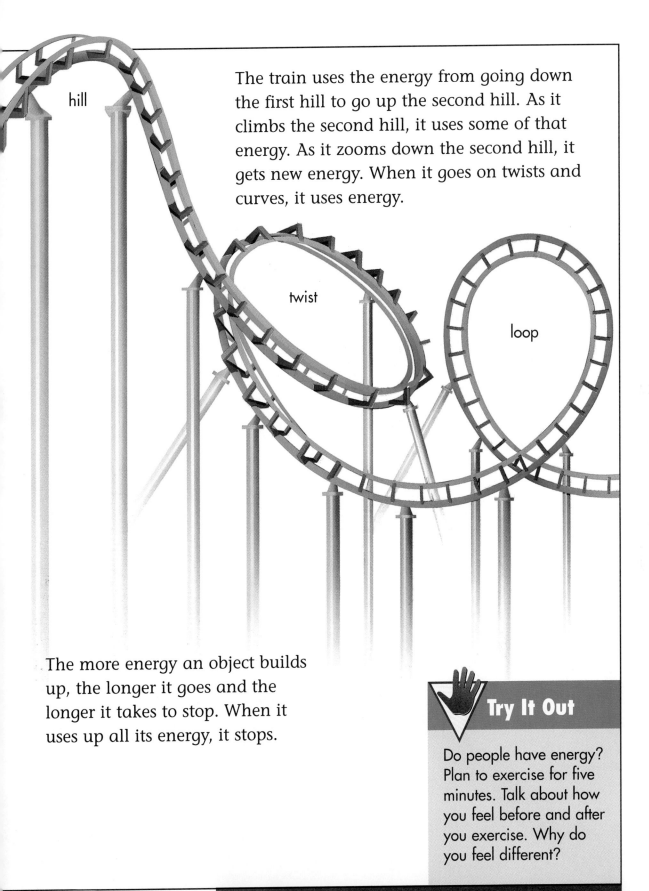

hill

The train uses the energy from going down the first hill to go up the second hill. As it climbs the second hill, it uses some of that energy. As it zooms down the second hill, it gets new energy. When it goes on twists and curves, it uses energy.

twist

loop

The more energy an object builds up, the longer it goes and the longer it takes to stop. When it uses up all its energy, it stops.

Try It Out

Do people have energy? Plan to exercise for five minutes. Talk about how you feel before and after you exercise. Why do you feel different?

What things affect how far a roller coaster goes?

A roller coaster runs on energy. Gravity and friction affect how a roller coaster runs.

Work with a group. Do an experiment to see how gravity, friction, and energy work.

Things You Need

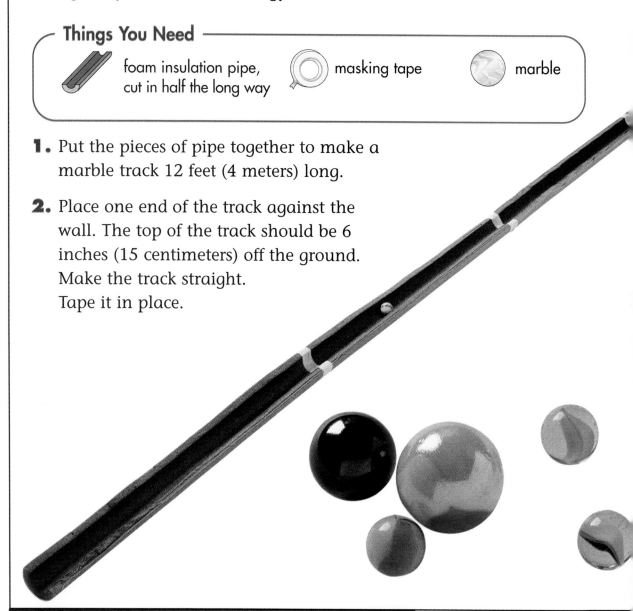

foam insulation pipe, cut in half the long way

masking tape

marble

1. Put the pieces of pipe together to make a marble track 12 feet (4 meters) long.

2. Place one end of the track against the wall. The top of the track should be 6 inches (15 centimeters) off the ground. Make the track straight.
   Tape it in place.

3. Put the marble at the top of the track. Let it roll down the track. Where does the marble stop? Mark the place with a piece of tape.

4. Roll the marble down the track again three times. Number each tape.

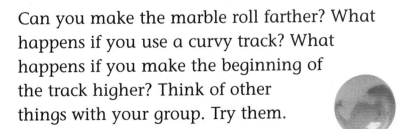

Can you make the marble roll farther? What happens if you use a curvy track? What happens if you make the beginning of the track higher? Think of other things with your group. Try them.

Write About It

Write a lab report showing what you did and your results.

What forces work together on a roller coaster?

Think about your ideal roller coaster. What would it look like? Would it have hills, loops, or curves? Work in a group to build your own marble coaster. Put all your ideas together. Start with the insulation pipe from the last experiment. Add any materials you have.

Roll your marble down the track. You may find the marble does not have enough energy to go all the way up the second hill. Together decide how you can make the marble build up more energy to make it go all the way to the end of the track.

Share what you learned with the class.

Write about the results.

My Record

Make a drawing of your roller coaster.

On our first roll, the marble stopped here:

We made these changes:

On our last roll, our marble stopped here:

❗ Talk About It

Work with your group to find places where forces of motion help your coaster work. Where can you see examples of friction or gravity at work?

Can a taller coaster give you a longer ride?

The chart shows the height and length of four roller coasters. Compare these numbers.

Roller Coaster	Place	Height of First Hill	Length of Track
American Eagle	Six Flags, IL	39 meters	1,400 meters
Colossus	Six Flags, CA	35 meters	1,300 meters
The Twister	Blitch Gardens, CO	30 meters	900 meters
The Riverside Cyclone	Riverside Park, MA	33 meters	1,000 meters

Answer these questions:

1. How long is the longest roller coaster?

2. How long is the roller coaster with the shortest first hill?

3. How does the height of the hill affect the length of the track?

What is the relationship between the height of the first hill and the length of the track?

1. Find how far each roller coaster goes for a meter of its height. For example, The Twister is 30 meters high and 900 meters long. You can find how far it goes for each meter of its height by dividing the height into the length. The Twister goes 30 meters for each meter of its height.

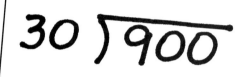

$$30 \overline{)900}$$

2. Find the answer for each of the coasters. When you have figured out each answer, find the average of all four. You will have the average distance a coaster travels for each meter of height.

Try It Out

Use the average distance for each meter of height. If you build a coaster with a hill that is 42 meters high, how far will the roller coaster go?

Riding the Scream Machine

Why do people love roller coasters? Why do they look for the exciting feeling they get as they zoom down the track?

Ask Michael Api. He started riding the roller coasters soon after he started to walk. By the age of nine, he had ridden 62 different roller coasters. His 14-year-old brother, Robert, has already ridden more than 140 coasters. The brothers want to ride even more roller coasters.

Other lovers of roller coasters take the same ride many times. Ask Richard Rodriguez. He rode Cyclone, a famous roller coaster at Coney Island in New York, for four days. Actually, he spent 103 hours and 55 minutes taking rides on the roller coaster.

That was a record. No one had ridden a coaster for such a long time.

Ask Carl Eichelman. He rode the famous Beast roller coaster at King's Island Park in Cincinnati, Ohio. He rode this scream machine 4,022 times during a five-year period. That's a lot of hours of thrills.

Many people are not as interested in roller coasters as Michael, Richard, and Carl.

But most riders like scary and exciting rides. As a result, new roller coasters are going up in many places.

These new coasters are even bigger and more exciting.

One example is the Dragon Mountain roller coaster. It is the highest steel coaster in North America. It is at Marineland Park in Niagara Falls, Canada. Riders go down a 186-foot (57-meter) drop and zoom around two vertical loops. The roller coaster passes through a copy of a volcano with lava inside it. Then it passes behind a small copy of Niagara Falls. The ride lasts only 3 minutes and 12 seconds, but it is full of excitement.

So if you ever get the chance, take that roller coaster ride. You may never want to get off.

Think About It

Think about how you would feel after riding a roller coaster for three days. Draw a picture of the way you would feel and share it with your classmates.

Using a Thesaurus

A **thesaurus** is a book that lists words that are alike in meaning. This part of a thesaurus has words that mean "to move."

A thesaurus can help you with your writing. You can find other words to use in place of a word that you have used again and again.

To move quickly

Dash means to move quickly. It often means to take a short, quick run.

The boy *dashed* to catch the bus.

Rush means to move quickly, often to get somewhere in time.

The passengers *rushed* to catch the train.

Zoom means to move at high speed, often in a car or other vehicle.

The cars *zoomed* down the highway.

To move slowly

Crawl means to move forward on one's hands and knees.

The baby *crawled* to get the toy.

Crawl can also mean to move slowly.

The cars *crawled* down the street.

Inch means to move very slowly, about an inch at a time.

We *inched* our way forward to the ticket booth.

Lumber means to move slowly, as if one were carrying a lot of weight.

The old truck *lumbered* up the mountain road.

Stroll means to walk slowly, usually when one has a lot of time and is not going to a particular place.

The family *strolled* through the park.

Write About It

Look back at the story "The Tug of War." Find the motion words on page 164. Which ones mean to move quickly? Which ones mean to move slowly?

Let's Twist Again

by Kal Mann

Let's twist again, like we did last summer.
Yeah, let's twist again, like we did last year.
Don't you remember when things were really humming?
Yeah, let's twist again, twisting time is here.

Yeah, around and around and up and down we go again.
O baby, make me know you love me so, and then
Let's twist again, like we did last summer.
Yeah, let's twist again, like we did last year.

▼ Talk About It

What parts of this song make you think of roller coasters?

Tell what you learned.

1. How do roller coasters work? What makes them move?

2. How can friction and gravity affect how a roller coaster works?

3. You are going to plan a roller coaster. How would it look? Draw a picture. Explain how it works.

4. Tell about one thing you learned about motion that you did not know before.

CHAPTER 10

Dealing with Change

Tell what you know.

What is happening in each picture?

How do you think each person feels?

Word Bank

angry

excited

happy

nervous

sad

scared

worried

FINISH LINE

 Talk About It

How would you feel in these situations? Would you feel comfortable or uncomfortable? Why?

CHAPTER 11

Handling Stress

What is stress?

Stress is what happens to your body when you are in a difficult situation. It happens when you feel a strong emotion. The emotion may be pleasant or unpleasant. You can feel signs of stress when you are worried, afraid, excited, or happy.

Everyone feels stress at one time or another. But things that cause you stress may not cause much stress to another person.

Stress can be helpful. When you run in a race, you want to win. The stress you feel helps you run faster. It makes you more alert.

Too much stress can be harmful to your body. Too much stress can make you tired and nervous. Too much stress makes it harder for your body to fight sickness.

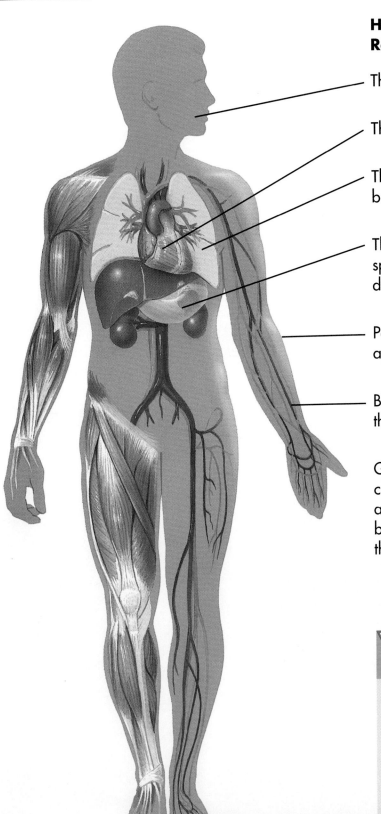

How Your Body Responds to Stress

The mouth may feel dry.

The heart may beat faster.

The lungs may breathe faster.

The stomach may speed up or slow down digesting food.

Perspiration may appear on the skin.

Blood may race through the body.

Glands may send a chemical called adrenaline through the body. The chemical gives the body energy.

Think About It

Why would happy feelings cause stress? Why would sad feelings cause stress? Why would problems cause stress?

What causes stress?

The changes people experience in life can cause stress.

Moving to a New Place

Moving to a new place can cause stress. You miss the family and friends you left behind. You have to learn new ways of doing things. You might even have to learn a new language.

Your whole family might feel stress. They may have to get new jobs. They may worry about money.

Going to a New School

Going to a new school can cause stress. You might worry about whether you will be able to do the schoolwork. You might worry about whether you will make friends. You might worry about whether the other students will like your clothes. If you speak a different language, you may worry whether you will understand the teacher and be able to study in English.

The stress in new situations does not have to be negative. You might see such changes as a chance to really do your best. The stress you feel might help you to do this.

Some Common Causes of Stress
Arguing with parents about rules
Arguing with brothers or sisters
Having a friendship begin or end
Having trouble with a school subject

Write About It

Make a list of things that have made you feel stress. Then put them in order. Write the thing that caused the most stress at the top.

How can you deal with stress?

Your room is a mess. You have a math test in two days. Your mother is mad at you because you were late getting home. You feel stressed out. There are many ways to handle too much stress. Here are three ideas.

Do breathing exercises.

One way of dealing with stress is to relax. This exercise will help you relax.

Breathe in. Count 1... 2... 3... 4...

Breathe out. Count 1... 2... 3... 4... 5... 6... 7... 8...

1. Sit or lie in a comfortable position.

2. Breathe in through your nose as deeply as you can. Count to four while you hold your breath.

3. Then breathe out through your mouth. Count to eight.

4. Do this exercise three or four times.

Make a list.

What are your problems? Make a list.

- Are there problems that you cannot do anything about? Try to forget them.

- Put the other problems in order. Try to deal with them one at a time.

Luke: Hey, Mom, I got 100 today!
Mom: That's great. What did you get 100 in?
Luke: Three subjects: a 30 in math, a 20 in history, and a 50 in English.

Try laughing.

Did you know that laughing can help you cut down on stress? Give a big smile and notice how the muscles in your face relax.

Try It Out

Find some jokes that make you laugh. Share one with a classmate. What is his or her response?

Ask for help.

Handling a problem by yourself can add to the stress you feel. Sometimes it helps to share your problem with someone else. Putting your problem into words can help you to see it in a new way.

Sometimes people write to the newspaper for advice. Read the following advice column from a newspaper.

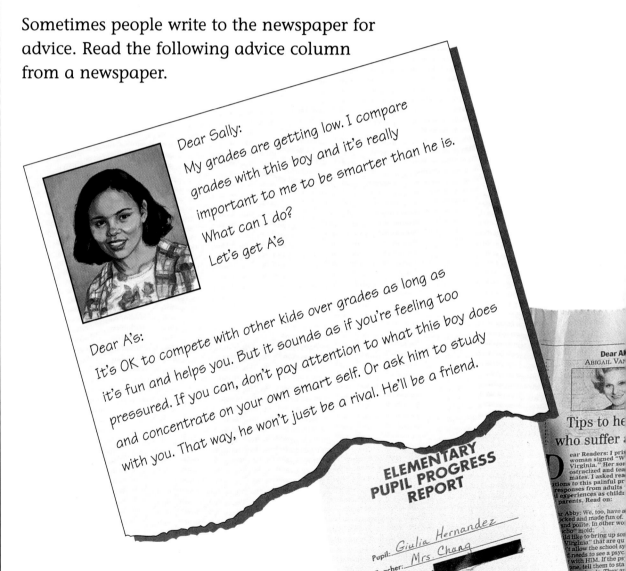

Dear Sally:

My grades are getting low. I compare grades with this boy and it's really important to me to be smarter than he is.

What can I do?

Let's get A's

Dear A's:

It's OK to compete with other kids over grades as long as it's fun and helps you. But it sounds as if you're feeling too pressured. If you can, don't pay attention to what this boy does and concentrate on your own smart self. Or ask him to study with you. That way, he won't just be a rival. He'll be a friend.

ELEMENTARY PUPIL PROGRESS REPORT

Pupil: _Giulia Hernandez_

Teacher: _Mrs. Chang_

Grade: _6_

ATTENDANCE	
1st Semester	2nd Semester
1	

Dear AI
ABIGAIL VAN

Tips to he
who suffer

ear Readers: I pri
woman signed "W
Virginia." Her son
ostracized and tea
mates. I asked rea
tions to this painful pr
responses from adults
experiences as childr
parents. Read on:

r Abby: We, too, have a
cked and made fun of.
nd polite. In other wo
cho" mold.
d like to bring up sor
Virginia" that are qu
't allow the school sy
d needs to see a psyc
with HIM. If the ps
ne, tell them to sta
e schools. They ar

y taxes. Your child
on-violent enviro
he administratio
ther parents. I
ve horror stories
ur child that he

Here is another letter to Sally:

Dear Sally:

I'm always worried that I've forgotten something big for school. I'm afraid I'll forget to do my homework. I am afraid that I'll forget to take my gym shoes to gym class. Please help!

G., almost 11

In the Year of the Boar and Jackie Robinson

by Bette Bao Lord

Reader's Tip
This reading is from a longer book. This part of the story tells of a young Chinese girl's first day at school in the United States. Her mother has taken her to the principal's office. Now the girl, Shirley, is going to meet her new teacher and classmates.

The principal then led her to class. The room was large, with windows up to the ceiling. Row after row of students, each one unlike the next. Some faces were white, like clean plates; others black like ebony. Some were in-between shades. A few were spotted all over. One boy was as big around as a water jar. Several others were as thin as chopsticks.

▲ Bette Bao Lord

No one wore a uniform of blue, like hers. There were sweaters with animals on them, shirts with stripes and shirts with squares, dresses in colors as varied as Grand-grand Uncle's paints. Three girls even wore earrings.

**Strategy Tip
Understand
Comparisons**
When Shirley sees her new classmates, she compares them to things she is familiar with from her home in China. A water jar is big and round. Chopsticks are thin wooden sticks used for eating.

**Strategy Tip
Stop and Think**
What things about the children's clothes surprise Shirley? Why do you think they surprise her?

Strategy Tip
Stop and Think
What is the principal
doing? What is she
telling the other
children?

Reader's Tip
Amitabha! is an
expression of surprise
that Shirley uses.

Reader's Tip
Shirley's mother said
that Shirley was an
ambassador. Shirley
was representing her
native country, China,
to people in the United
States. So that's why
Shirley calls herself
an ambassador. Here
Shirley is thinking that
she would like a pair of
high-heeled shoes so
that she would be tall
like the other children.

Strategy Tip
Stop and Think
What did Shirley guess?

While Shirley looked about, the principal had
been making a speech. Suddenly it ended with
"Shirley Temple Wong." The class stood up and
waved.

Amitabha! They were all so tall. Even Water
Jar was a head taller than she. For a fleeting
moment she wondered if Mother would
consider buying an ambassador a pair of
high-heeled shoes.

"Hi, Shirley!" The
class shouted.

Shirley bowed
deeply. Then,
taking a guess,
she replied, "Hi!"

The teacher introduced herself and showed the new pupil to a front-row seat. Shirley liked her right away, although she had a most difficult name, Mrs. Rappaport. She was a tiny woman with dainty bones and fiery red hair brushed skyward. Shirley thought that in her previous life she must have been a bird, a cardinal perhaps. Yet she commanded respect, for no student talked out of turn.

Language Tip
Vocabulary
Dainty means "tiny."

Language Tip
Vocabulary
A cardinal is a red bird. The feathers on the top of its head rise up to a point.

Language Tip
Idiom
To talk out of turn means "to talk when you are not allowed to talk."

Throughout the lessons, Shirley leaned forward, barely touching her seat, to catch the meaning, but the words sounded like gurgling water. Now and then, when Mrs. Rappaport looked her way, she opened and shut her eyes as the principal had done, to show friendship.

At lunchtime, Shirley went with the class to the school cafeteria, but before she could pick up a tray, several boys and girls waved for her to follow them. They were smiling, so she went along.

Reader's Tip
The principal had winked at Shirley to make her feel comfortable. Now Shirley thinks that it is a good thing to wink at people. But Shirley closes both eyes, instead of one, when she winks.

They snuck back to the classroom to pick up coats, then hurried out the door and across the school yard to a nearby store. Shirley was certain they should not be there, but what choice did she have? These were now her friends.

Strategy Tip
Put Yourself in the Story
Shirley thinks that the other students are doing something wrong, but she decides to follow them. What would you do?

One by one they gave their lunch money to the store owner, whom they called "Mr. P." In return, he gave each a bottle of orange-colored water, bread twice the size of an ear of corn oozing with meat balls, peppers, onions, and hot red gravy, and a large piece of brown paper to lay on the icy sidewalk and sit upon.

CONNECT LANGUAGE • HEALTH/LITERATURE

While they ate, everyone except Shirley played marbles or cards and traded bottle caps and pictures of men swinging a stick or wearing one huge glove. It was the best lunch Shirley had ever had.

Reader's Tip
The pictures of men swinging a bat and wearing gloves are baseball cards. These cards have pictures of major league baseball players and information about these players. Many children collect these cards.

Strategy Tip
Put Yourself in the Story
Why do you think that Shirley says it is the best lunch she ever had?

Schools in Japan and the United States

by Sayo Yamaguchi

Reader's Tip
This story was written by a young girl from Japan who is going to school in the United States. She tells her ideas about the differences between Japanese schools and schools in the United States.

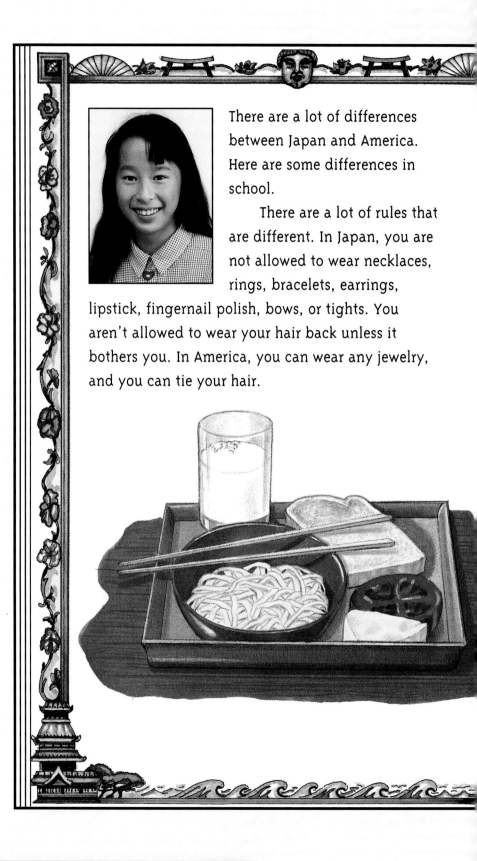

There are a lot of differences between Japan and America. Here are some differences in school.

There are a lot of rules that are different. In Japan, you are not allowed to wear necklaces, rings, bracelets, earrings, lipstick, fingernail polish, bows, or tights. You aren't allowed to wear your hair back unless it bothers you. In America, you can wear any jewelry, and you can tie your hair.

There are a lot of things that are different about lunchtime. In Japan, you have to eat your lunch at your desk. You can't bring lunch. You have to buy your lunch. There is a lot of food, and you have to eat all the lunch! You can't throw it away! In America, you don't have to eat all the lunch. You can throw it away. You can bring lunch from home, or you can buy lunch. You eat in the gym in America.

There are a lot of differences in elementary school. In Japan, you wear uniforms to school on Monday, Tuesday, Wednesday, Thursday, and Friday. You go to school for three hours on Saturday, but you don't have to wear your uniform. You usually go to kindergarten for three years. In America, you only go to kindergarten for a year. You don't go to school on Saturday, and you don't wear uniforms either.

In Japan, vacations are short. In winter and spring, you only have one or two weeks. In summer, you have one or two months. In America, you have more vacations. In winter, there are two weeks. Spring vacation is about one week. In summer, you have three months.

There are a lot of differences between schools in America and Japan. I think I am lucky to be a part of both countries.

Study Tip
Compare and Contrast
Writers often compare and contrast things. In this essay, the student contrasts school in Japan with school in the United States. What things about school in the two countries does she compare?

You Can Do Better

by Kalli Dakos

I did my best,
But the teacher wrote,
In bright red,
"You can do better."

Now I'm sitting here
Wondering,
How can I do better
Than my best?

Tell what you learned.

1. How does the body react to stress? What happens?

2. What situations can cause stress?

3. How can you deal with stress?

4. Think over the story. What problems did Shirley have on her first day of school in a new country? Did you have similar problems?

5. What is the most important thing you learned in this chapter?

CHAPTER 12

Getting Information

Tell what you know.

What sources of information do people use?

What changes have there been in the ways people can get information?

Talk About It

What sources of information do you use? Why do you use those sources of information? What sources of information do you use in English?

216

Encyclopedias

When you need the answer to almost any question, look in an encyclopedia. An encyclopedia is a good **reference tool.** It has information about a large number of topics. It has information about people, places, and things. It is full of facts. It has a great deal of information on events and people who lived in the past.

Roosevelt, Franklin Delano (1882–1945)
Franklin Delano Roosevelt was the 32nd president of the United States. He served longer than any other president—over 12 years—from 1933 to 1945. He was called "FDR" for short.

He was born in 1882, in Hyde Park, New York, to a wealthy family. In 1921, he got sick with polio. Even though he was crippled for life and could no longer walk well, he went on to do great things. He was one of America's greatest presidents.

He led the United States through the Great Depression, a time when millions of people had no jobs and little money. He said, "The only thing we have to fear is fear itself." He started many government programs, such as Social Security, that helped older people and sick people.

As commander-in-chief, he led the United States on its way to victory in World War II.

He died suddenly of a cerebral hemorrhage in 1945.

Try It Out

What encyclopedias are in your school or local library? Are there any picture encyclopedias?

How is information organized in an encyclopedia?

Use an encyclopedia to find out about another famous American who overcame a disability. Look up Helen Keller. (Look under *K*.) When did she live? What disabilities did she have? What did she accomplish?

Magazines

Magazines come out every week or every month. The information they have is more recent than the information in encyclopedias. Articles are written in an interesting way to attract the reader. Often it is fun just to look at the pictures in a magazine.

Many magazines focus on one subject area. For example, there are magazines with articles only about sports. There are magazines for students of your age.

A Real Success Story

Success, then a problem, then success. That's the story of Gloria Estefan, singer with the hit group Miami Sound Machine.

The Cuban-born singer and songwriter became famous in the 1980s. Her group attracted millions of listeners with the sounds of Hispanic dance music.

Then Estefan was in a terrible car accident. Her back was broken.

Doctors operated and put two metal rods down Estefan's back. Estefan was in constant pain. She says that she was depressed only once. "The beginning was the worst, the low point." She could only lift her foot an inch off the ground.

Slowly she managed to walk on her own. Now she is back on stage singing and dancing. And her albums sell thousands of copies.

Try It Out

Go to a school or local library. Look at the magazines. Are there any magazines that interest you? What are they?

Newspapers

The newspaper has information about events that are currently happening.

Volcano Erupts and Travel Is Disrupted

NEW ZEALAND—
September 26

Mount Ruapehu has begun to throw out ash, steam, and rocks the size of cars. Dr. Sidney Simons, a geologist and expert on volcanoes, told reporters that a major eruption could occur at any time. He has asked the government to take action to keep people safe.

The government has stopped certain kinds of travel. Airplanes are not allowed to fly near the mountain because the ash may clog their engines, causing the engines to stop working. Train travel in the area has been stopped because the train track runs near the side of the mountain. Ash and mud could fall on the tracks.

People in the area can expect heavy ash to fall. One local resident told reporters, "I'm leaving! It's too stressful to stay here any longer." Many more people may decide to leave the area.

News stories give facts. They answer the following questions:

Who is in the story?
What happened?
Where did it happen?
When did it happen?
Why did it happen?

Newspapers have sections in addition to news sections. They have sports and business sections. They also have feature sections. The articles in feature sections are a lot like the articles in magazines.

Talk About It

What kind of article is the one on page 222? Find a current newspaper. Pick an article that interests you. Find the who, what, where, when, and why.

Write to learn.

Writing down information you read is useful. Writing can help you remember ideas. Thinking about the connections between ideas can help you understand what you read better.

Graphic organizers can help you organize pieces of information and find connections between them.

This graphic organizer has main topics about the life of Franklin Roosevelt: Early Life, Problems, Accomplishments. Under each topic is related information.

Franklin Roosevelt		
Early Life	**Problems**	**Accomplishments**
• born in 1882 • from rich family	• got polio • had trouble walking	• elected President for four terms • led the United States through bad economic times • led nation through World War II

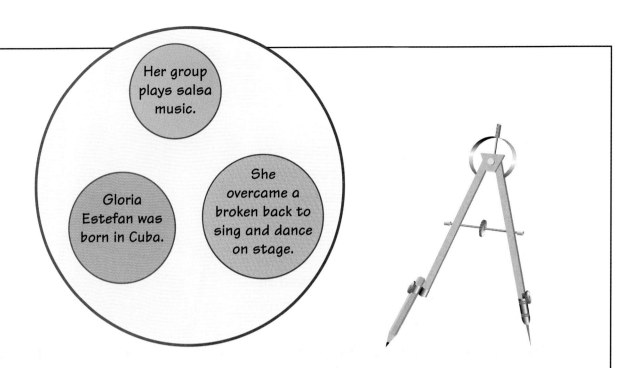

Sometimes it is helpful just to write down four or five facts that you find interesting about something you have read. This graphic organizer has facts about Gloria Estefan.

Write About It

Look at the newspaper article on page 222. Use a graphic organizer to remember important information from it.

Choose a topic that interests you. Find an encyclopedia, magazine, or newspaper article about it. Write down important or interesting information from it in a graphic organizer.

Interviews

Writers of newspapers and magazines use interviews to get information. They ask questions of famous people or people in the news.

This reading is taken from a book of interviews of young people who moved to the United States. Jorge, a sixteen-year-old Cuban boy, is speaking of his family.

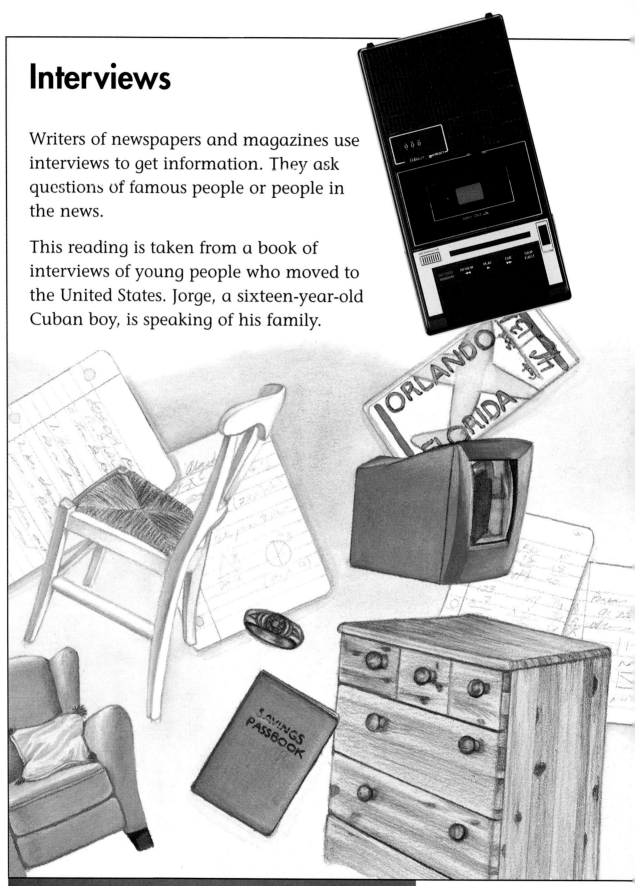

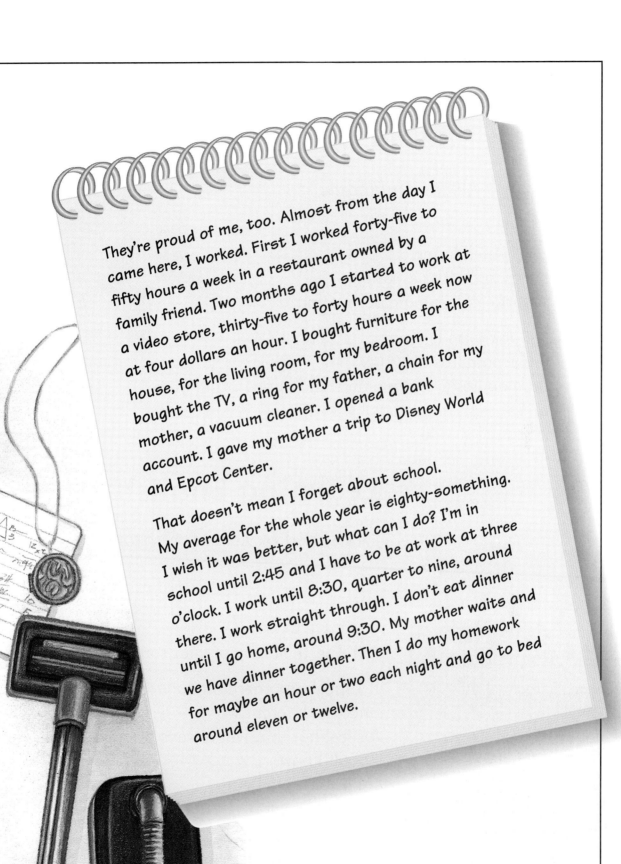

They're proud of me, too. Almost from the day I came here, I worked. First I worked forty-five to fifty hours a week in a restaurant owned by a family friend. Two months ago I started to work at a video store, thirty-five to forty hours a week now at four dollars an hour. I bought furniture for the house, for the living room, for my bedroom. I bought the TV, a ring for my father, a chain for my mother, a vacuum cleaner. I opened a bank account. I gave my mother a trip to Disney World and Epcot Center.

That doesn't mean I forget about school. My average for the whole year is eighty-something. I wish it was better, but what can I do? I'm in school until 2:45 and I have to be at work at three o'clock. I work until 8:30, quarter to nine, around there. I work straight through. I don't eat dinner until I go home, around 9:30. My mother waits and we have dinner together. Then I do my homework for maybe an hour or two each night and go to bed around eleven or twelve.

Aprender el inglés

by Luis Albero Ambroggio

Vida
para entenderme
tienes que saber español
sentirlo en la sangre de tu alma.

Si hablo otro lenguaje
y uso palabras distintas
para expresar sentimientos que nunca cambiarán
no sé
si seguiré siendo
la misma persona.

Learning English

Translated by Lori M. Carlson

Life
to understand me
you have to know Spanish
feel it in the blood of your soul.

If I speak another language
and use different words
for feelings that will always stay the same
I don't know
If I'll continue being
the same person.

? Think About It

The author of the poem says that he can only express himself completely in his native language. Do you have trouble getting information in English? What ways can you help yourself get information?

Tell what you learned.

1. What sources of information did you use as you studied this chapter? What was the most interesting thing you read?

2. What is the most important thing you learned on your own as you studied this chapter?

Writer's Workshop

Follow these steps to be a good writer.

① Prewriting

Choose a topic.
List your ideas.
Ask friends for ideas.
Look in books for ideas.

cities   jobs

coming to America   planets

computers   sounds

dinosaurs   sports

food   TV

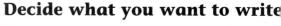

Decide what you want to write
Do you want to write a story?
Do you want to explain something?
Do you want to describe something
Do you want to tell how you feel?

Focus your topic.

Use a graphic organizer.
Focus on one idea.

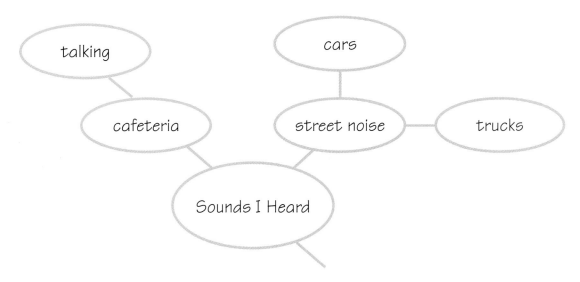

Find details about your topic.

Look for information in books
and magazines.
Ask people for information.
Think about how things look,
sound, feel, and taste.

② Drafting

Get what you need.
Get paper and pencils.
Get your graphic organizer.
Sit in a comfortable place.

Set a goal.
How much will you write now?

Read your notes.
What do you want to say first?

Keep writing.
Write down all your ideas.
Don't worry about spelling and punctuation now.

Sounds I Heard

I see many cars and truks on the streets
Some cars were honking ther horns. I saw
a tall building too.
      At school, the peeple in the cafeteria were
very noisy they was talking. In muzic class,
everyone was singing. After school, I walked by
a park. the grant Park Orchestra was playing
muzic there I liked the drums and the trupets.
      I want play the the drums some day. I like
Loud sounds.

③ Revising

Read what you wrote. Ask yourself:
Does my story have a beginning,
a middle, and an end?
Is my information correct?
What parts should I keep?
What parts should I leave out?

"I think I need a better beginning."

Talk with someone.
Show your writing to a friend or your teacher.
Do your readers understand your writing?

"Why did you tell about a tall building?"

Proofreading

Check your spelling.
Look in a dictionary or ask for help.

Look for capital letters.

Look for correct punctuation.

Make a new copy.

≡ **Make a capital.**

╱ **Make a small letter.**

∧ **Add something.**

℘ **Take out something.**

⊙ **Add a period.**

⌙ **Make a new paragraph.**

Sounds I Heard

Yesterday I hear many sounds. I see many cars and truks on the streets. Some cars were honking ther horns.
At school, the people in the cafeteria were very noisy, they was talking. In muzic class, everyone was singing. After school, I walked by a park. the grant Park Orchestra was playing muzic there. I liked the drums and the trupets. I want play the the drums some day. I like loud sounds.

⑤ Presenting

Share your writing.
Read it aloud to your family or classmates.
Make a book. Lend the book to your family
or classmates.

Sounds I Heard

Yesterday I heard many sounds. I saw many cars
and trucks on the streets. Some cars were honking
their horns.

At school, the people in the cafeteria were very
noisy. They were talking. In music class, everyone
was singing.

After school, I walked by a park. The Grant Park
Orchestra was playing music there. I liked the drums
and the trumpets.

I want to play the drums some day. I like
loud sounds.

What a Good Writer Can Do

- I can plan before I write.

- I can write about things I know. I can write about my family, my school, and myself.

- I can write stories with a beginning, a middle, and an end.

- I can ask others to read my work.

- I can write in complete sentences.

- I can put periods at the ends of sentences.

- I can make my handwriting easy to read.